IN BED WITH THE BADGE

IN BED WITH THE BADGE

THE BARBARA SHEEHAN STORY

Jennifer Sheehan Joyce and Raymond M. Sheehan

CHANGING LIVES PRESS

Changing Lives Press
50 Public Square #1600
Cleveland, OH 44113
www.changinglivespress.com

Library of Congress Cataloging-in-Publication Data is available
through the Library of Congress.

ISBN-13: 978-09843047-1-4
ISBN-10: 09843047-1-1

Editor: Shari Johnson
Cover and interior design: Gary A. Rosenberg

Printed in the United States of America

10   9   8   7   6   5   4   3   2   1

Contents

In memory of all who have been killed by their abusers,
to those who have had the courage to survive abuse,
to Mom for never losing faith, and most of all,
to God for listening.

Acknowledgments

THIS BOOK HAS BEEN VERY DIFFICULT FOR US TO WRITE. Our story is not easily shared, but we feel it will help others and that is very important to us. It is our faith and belief in God that has allowed us to get to this point in our lives. Of course, we owe it mostly to Mom. And although it would not be possible to name every one of you, the incredible support, prayers, encouragement and love that you have given us throughout this terrible time have sustained us when we thought we couldn't go on. You have blessed our lives beyond words. How can we ever thank you enough?

Raymond M. Sheehan

On Monday, February 18, 2008, my life changed forever; changed for the better. At 12:45 in the afternoon, my mother shot and killed my father. I was relieved—relieved that he hadn't killed her, and relieved that he was dead.

I had a 12:30 class that day at Sacred Heart University in Fairfield, Connecticut. I had left my phone in my dorm room, and when I returned at around two o'clock, there were ten texts from my sister, Jennifer. They all said essentially the same thing: "Where are you?" "Why aren't you answering me?" The final text said, "I am coming up there to pick you up." I panicked. I thought for sure that my mother must be dead—why else would Jen be coming to get me? When I was finally able to speak with her, I asked her repeatedly to put our mom on the phone, but she just kept saying, "I can't . . . I can't." I knew that my dad had finally killed my mom. He had told her, Jen and me enough times that he would, and he had severely injured my mom more times than I could count.

During the time before Jen arrived, I could only imagine what had happened, and I thought the worst. As soon as Jen drove up with my mom's cousin Frankie, she got out of the car and said, "Dad is dead and Mom killed him." It was a huge relief—I felt that a weight had been taken off my shoulders.

Sometime after noon that same day, Jen had received a call at work from her friend Christie who lives across the street from our house in Queens, New York. Jen was working at Sloan-Kettering, about to receive her bachelor's degree in nursing in May. Christie told her that she had to come home. Jen explained to her that she had taken the train to work and Christie said, "You don't understand, get into a cab and come home!" Christie had seen Mom taken away by the police, so she knew what had happened, but she didn't want to tell Jen on the phone.

Jen freaked out, just as I had—she thought Mom was dead. One of the nurses gave her money for the cab and she called her boyfriend, Jesse, who is now her husband. He said, "Don't go in the house—he might kill you."

Christie waited for her around the corner because she didn't want the cab to stop in front of the house. She got in the cab and said, "Your mom's okay. Let's go to your grandparents' house and they will tell you everything." Our grandparents live only a few blocks from our house. When they got there, Jen was so upset that she fell as she was getting out of the cab and couldn't walk. When she went inside the house, because our grandparents weren't upset or crying, she knew Mom must be okay. She felt relieved when she found out what happened, but she was afraid that I would see something on the news about it before she could tell me, and she wasn't sure if she should tell me over the phone. Mom's cousin Frankie and a few other people were at our grandparents' house, and when Jen said she wanted to pick me up, Frankie told her to get in the car and he would drive her.

The ride back home was quiet. We knew mom had been arrested and we talked about seeing her as soon as possible, but then there was so much to think about. We were trying to come to grips with what had happened . . . and there were so many memories.

PROLOGUE

―――――――

Living in Limbo

"This only is denied to God: the power to undo the past."
—AGATHON

On that fateful day when I was told that something terrible had happened at home, I thought my mother was dead—that my dad had followed through on his constant threats and had killed her. When I heard that Mom was not the one who had died, I was immensely relieved and thanked God. Our focus then became getting her released from jail. My brother, Raymond, and I went to the police station thinking that we could see her free from our father for the first time, but she had been taken to the hospital because her blood pressure was so high and she was having heart palpitations.

Our grandparents had found a lawyer, a decent man who practiced in Orange County, in Upstate New York. We were told that Mom wouldn't be remanded (held in custody). Our thinking was, *Why would they keep her anyway, wasn't this OBVIOUSLY self-defense?* We couldn't wait to get her released.

1

Raymond and I stayed at Nanni and Poppop's (Mom's parents) house that night. Neither of us got much sleep, if any. We still couldn't believe that this had happened. Were we really finally free from the monster that we were so afraid would kill our mother? We didn't know very much about the prison system, and didn't know what to expect. The arraignment was to be the following morning.

Although we were relieved to see with our own eyes that she was okay, seeing Mom for the first time since the shooting was heartbreaking. Hadn't all the years of hell been enough? And why wasn't this an obvious case of self-defense? She was in the Queens County Court House awaiting her arraignment. She was sobbing and kept saying she was sorry. Why was she sorry? I think she felt that she had let us down—she hadn't. How could our mom, the gentlest person on the face of the earth, be standing there in hand-cuffs? And why was she sorry that she had killed a monster?

We waited for hours, watching as other people were arraigned. Then it was finally her turn. Mom had been charged with second-degree murder, which could be a sentence of from twenty-five years to life, and a second felony charge of two counts of illegal possession of a firearm—firearms that were legally owned by our father. We couldn't believe what we were hearing when the prose-cutor *did* ask for remand, and our attorney wasn't prepared with a rebuttal. This wasn't the way it was supposed to happen. She clearly had been defending herself. But that was only the first blow—the second one came when the judge denied bail and fol-lowed that with an order for an immediate transfer to Rikers Island for processing. He then banged his gavel and just like that, it was over. We were stunned. It all happened so fast that for a moment I lost my equilibrium—I felt as though I had been spun around a hundred times, then forced to stand still and walk.

I wanted so badly just to hug her, but of course that wasn't possible. I knew Mom was trying to hold it together. As always, she was trying to be strong for our benefit. She told us much later that she had collapsed once she was behind the door where we could no longer see her. She fell to the floor, hysterically sobbing over what had just taken place inside the courtroom.

It was hard to grasp that within a mere 24 hours she had gone through the horror of kill or be killed, been arrested, cuffed, booked and held without bail. It felt like a good dream and a bad dream rolled into one; but a dream that surely I would wake from.

When we left the courthouse there were reporters everywhere. We had no idea it would be of such interest to the media—but then that was the last thing on our minds.

The attorney could not secure an appeal date to reargue for bail for another nine days. We felt that a change in attorneys was necessary. We had first seen Michael Dowd on television commenting on Mom's case as a guest expert in domestic violence cases. After investigating him, we were convinced he was the man for the job. The "Barbara Sheehan entourage"—which consisted of our grandparents; Mom's sister, Robin, and her husband, Mike; Mom's brother, Michael, and his wife, Allison; Mom's cousin Frankie; Raymond; my boyfriend, Jesse, and me—met with Mr. Dowd at his office in Manhattan. He greeted us with, "I was hoping you would call."

After speaking with Mr. Dowd, our hopes were higher, and Raymond and I went to Rikers to see Mom. We had looked up the visiting hours on the computer. She wasn't behind glass and we were finally able to hug her. She kept saying, "I'm sorry . . . I'm sorry." Raymond told her that she had done the right thing and had saved all of our lives. I, of course, agreed.

Hiring Mr. Dowd proved to be a step in the right direction, as he was able to have Mom released on bail—the judge set it at one million dollars. It took our family several days to come up with the money. Four houses were mortgaged: Mom's childhood home, which was still occupied by Nanni and Poppop, plus the homes owned by her brother, sister, and aunt.

Mom was released twelve days after the incident. It was a Saturday night—ten o'clock to be exact. Poppop was there with Raymond and me, standing outside in the freezing air, both literally and figuratively. This wasn't fair and it wasn't turning out as it should. We embraced Mom with the warmth and love that for years our father had told her she didn't deserve. It felt great and it was comforting, but we knew this wasn't the end.

Mom then asked us about the funeral arrangements. I told her that we had gone to the wake. It's hard to explain, but when you have a monster like him in your life for over 18 years, you have to see for yourself.

Raymond said, "We went to make sure he was really dead."

After Mom was released on bail and we were able to talk, she told us how she felt when she was taken to Rikers. Once she got to Rikers, instead of breaking down as she was sure she would, she said she had a sense of security she hadn't felt since the abuse began. The hardest part for her was the separation from us.

She told us of a kind nun who made rounds and distributed Bibles. She gave Mom a Bible and a rosary to give her comfort. Ironically, Rikers provided Mom with a sense of freedom she hadn't possessed through the years of being married to our father. She could now reach out to others for help—and could receive that help. If she had ever tried to get help, not only would he have killed her, but Raymond and me as well. He could make all of us feel helpless with just one look. If not that, he would tell us that we had nowhere to turn, no one to tell. He constantly reminded us that we couldn't call the police because he *was* the police. He would whisper to me in a bone chilling voice that if Mom were ever to leave him, he would kill all of us. For Mom, it was a daily grind of physical and emotional abuse with no way out.

We weren't surprised that her main concern was about us—she felt that we had already suffered too much, and for that reason she wanted this to go away as soon as possible. This is what was so frustrating for all of us—we had to make certain that the prosecution understood this. However, it was over three years before her case went to trial. In a way, that was good—it felt almost as if it had gone away and we could lead some sort of a normal life.

Mom had numerous meetings with the judge from March 2008 to December 2009: March 28, April 29, June 4, July 23, September 11, October 28, December 1, January 14, February 23, March 10, April 8, April 14, April 27, June 12, July 23, July 30, September 23, September 30, October 21, October 29, November 11, and December 9. These were difficult, because the judge didn't attempt to hide his disdain for her.

Then, by some intervention of grace, that judge retired. However, he didn't leave before issuing an inconceivable ruling; the disallowance of expert testimony that was the very essence of Mom's defense—that she was a battered woman and had been profession- ally diagnosed with battered woman syndrome. Without expert testimony, her right to a defense was as good as gone. There would be no way to prove that she shot my father in self-defense; that her life was in imminent danger that day; and that it was either her life or his.

Of course Mr. Dowd appealed this ruling, but it was five months before the decision was made. Mom said she was driving home from work when Mr. Dowd called to tell her that the appeal was denied. She told me how devastated she was; that it felt like the abuse was never going to end. I knew how bad it was for her when she said at that point she thought maybe she should have just let him kill her. I had wished every day that I could take the abuse myself and give her a break. I know my brother had felt this way too.

She said she had felt dizzy, and pulled over to the side of the road. She wasn't sure that she could drive herself home, so she called her social worker, Josie. This woman has been a Godsend to us. She assisted in Mom's case as a therapist, a battered woman advocate, and she has become a trusted friend. She is the one who told Mom about the controversial disorder known as battered woman syndrome. Who could have understood what losing this appeal meant to Mom more than Josie? The prosecution could have built an undisputed case against her, supporting their theory that the timid school secretary and battered mother of two was nothing more than a cold-blooded murderer; that she planned to kill her husband; and that she was hiding behind a bogus illness diagnosed by pseudo-professionals to help her get away with it.

Josie, as always, came through for her. She calmed her down and told Mom to appeal again, to a higher court. She told her that Mr. Dowd would take care of it, and he did. He appealed to the New York State Court of Appeals, but that meant the upcoming court date set for Mom's trial would be another postponement.

Sometimes in a situation such as ours, one has to look for the bright side of things. This meant that Mom was there to walk me down the aisle at my wedding and go to my college graduation as I received my Bachelor of Science in Nursing degree. She got to see Raymond play his final college football seasons, as well as graduate from college. Mom always supported us in anything we did, and she had been watching Raymond play sports since he was big enough to throw or catch a ball. The sport didn't matter, as long as it wasn't basketball. Our father's vicious bullying when he coached Raymond's grade school team had made the sport detestable to both Raymond and my mom. Unfortunately, the meanness and bullying weren't isolated to the court.

A Note from the Author

Ithink it's true of most kids that we don't spend much time thinking about what our parents' lives were like before we came into the picture until we are grown—if even then. But in our case our lives were so full of fear, anxiety, worry and just trying to survive, it never occurred to us to wonder why someone as kind, gentle and loving as our mother would have ever married our father. Once I was able to grasp that we were safe and we could think about other things, I asked Mom if she would tell me about her life before he was in the picture, and what had attracted her to him.

I now have the whole picture—even the parts Raymond and I weren't aware of as we were growing up. We've spent many precious hours together, talking about this—something we were unable to do while my father was alive. Much of what I learned was difficult to hear, but knowing it now makes me admire my mother even more.

As you read this book, my hope is that if you become aware of danger signs that you are currently ignoring in your own life, you will get out—you will get help before it is too late—before there is a tragedy.

—Jennifer Sheehan Joyce

CHAPTER ONE

The Attraction

*"The deepest definition of youth
is life as yet untouched by tragedy."*
—ALFRED NORTH WHITEHEAD

When Mom first saw my father, she was convinced that there was no way he could ever notice her, as he was too busy being the life of the party. It was summertime, and Dad's brother Danny had just been ordained a priest. My mom's family had been invited to the reception celebration at Del Montes in Brooklyn. Danny had been a deacon and would now be a priest at their parish, Our Lady of Grace; the same parish where my grandfather ran the youth sports program. This wedding hall was grand, and in the vein of most traditional New York–style reception halls, everything was big: big band, big food, big bar, and larger-than-life people. My mother thought my dad was no exception.

The first time there was any interaction between my parents, he was telling a joke to a group of friends, and Mom laughed. She knew of him. Danny had mentioned that he had a younger brother whom she might find fun and interesting, and she had a sneaking suspicion that Danny had informed Dad of her existence as well. She was flattered to think so, since she was only seventeen, while this college boy named Ray had turned Danny's guests into his own personal audience. He could have had them paying for front-row seats—he was that good. Of course he absolutely loved the attention; how they hung on every word and every pause as he casually lifted his drink to his lips.

Like the others, Mom was immediately drawn to this fun-loving guy who seemed to have that very attractive attribute called confidence—but not so much that he was cocky. Dressed in a three-piece navy blue suit and sporting a red carnation on his lapel, Mom said he had the charisma of a young Sinatra; although a half-Italian, half-Irish Sinatra. His hand gestures were in sync with his inflections, which were always timed perfectly and made for well-delivered punch lines and convincing talking points. He wasn't too loud or obnoxious, but was still very much the quintessential Brooklynite in those days—a tall, olive-skinned, average-looking, sharply dressed fast-talker with a grand plan for his life: Become a cop. New York City's Finest. NYPD.

He was already enrolled in college at John Jay, which everyone knew had a reputation for its outstanding criminal law program. If someone were entering the law field, whether as an officer or attorney, and they were worth their salt, chances are they would head into Manhattan from whatever borough they hailed from and proudly join the student body of John Jay.

As his *audience* dispersed, he turned his full attention on my mother. "So, you liked that joke? Or are you the type of girl who laughs at anything?"

"I am not the type of girl who is any type of girl." She was proud of sounding more self-confident than she actually felt around this smooth, older guy.

"Well, clearly you *are* the type of girl who knows a funny joke when she hears one. And that's important."

This flirtatious repartee made my mother feel older than she was. High school guys her age weren't big on verbal exchanges. Taking the challenge, she gave my dad her best comeback with something like, "I guess that depends on who it's important to."

Whatever she said made him laugh and hearing him laugh made her laugh, too. Mom liked to laugh and this made her like him even more. Then to top it all off, *If I Can't Have You,* one of her favorite hits from the *Fever* sound track, was playing as Dad swept a hand toward the dance floor as if he owned it and would love nothing better than to share it with her.

They ended up dancing the night away.

My dad called her the very next day and that just blew her away. After all, a modest, Catholic high school girl from Howard Beach catching the eye of a college boy was something to brag to her friends about. But still she worried that she might have come off too strong at the party. She wasn't quite sure what got into her, flirting with him like that. She wondered if she couldn't sustain the impression she must have given him just the evening before, would he even like the person who was now on the phone?

"Hi, Barbara. It's Ray. Danny Sheehan's brother. Or should I say *Father* Danny's brother?"

His light-hearted opening was laced with a slight quiver in his voice. Mom wondered if the man who was so confident last night might be a little less sure of himself today.

"Hello, Father Danny's brother," she replied.

Crouched in the corner of the kitchen, Mom nervously twirled the yellow curly phone cord in the opposite direction, trying to see how long it would take before she could tame it straight.

It seemed to her that Dad was sincerely interested in getting to know her better. Did she like movies? What about hobbies? How did she spend her spare time? Was she planning on going to college? Not only was he inquisitive, he was listening closely to the answers. Mom told me that none of the high school boys had ever listened to her like that before, so naturally she was impressed. He followed up with more questions until he got to the biggie: Did she have a boyfriend?

Mom dated a lot, but she didn't have a special boyfriend at that time, and she was happy to say, "Nope. No boyfriend. I mean, nobody that I am romantic about."

"Well, Barbara, it was nice talking to you."

His abrupt close to the conversation left her off-balance. Lacking self-confidence, my mom concluded that she had said something immature and foolish or giggled too much or had come off too eager. She was quite surprised when he called a few days later. Again, his small talk went on and on as she paced the kitchen, wondering why he didn't just ask her out. Instead, the dance continued:

What kind of music did she like? Disco? Great, him too. Was she close with her family? While they weren't exactly the Waltons, they were close, and that was something he could also relate to.

When he asked if, since she liked discos, had she ever been to the Copacabana, Mom thought, *Finally, a date! And what should I wear to the Copacabana?*

But . . . no. For two weeks the calls came, with Dad doing his Q&A for the duration of each and every phone call. Confused by his mixed signals, Mom confided in her best friend, Annie, about the lengthy chats that were seemingly going nowhere. Was there something strange about this guy, or was she off base with her own expectations? Annie came up with the perfect explanation. He must have borrowed some "liquid courage" at the party and that gave him the nerve to make a play for her that night. Even if he hadn't come on as strong since then, he had to like her to keep calling so much and a smart girl would be patient for a guy who was clearly worth the wait.

And Mom was patient. The marathon phone calls seemed to go on indefinitely, but she did come to appreciate learning so much about this college boy who came from such a decent family. To have a priest in the family is an honor; a status symbol that indicates the parents have done something right in the raising and rearing of their brood. However, she said that Dad didn't put on lofty airs about it, and she liked him even more for humanizing his upbringing. He told her about the boisterousness of their family conversations at dinner; how they spoke to one another so loudly sometimes that the neighbors actually thought they were arguing. They always ate fish on Christmas Eve, because his mother's Italian family had kept that tradition alive from the time they arrived on Ellis Island from Calabria, Italy, two generations before. In addition to his older brother Danny, he had a fraternal twin brother, Vincent. According to my mother, she felt that there was a lot to like about my father, but what she liked most of all was how committed he was to becoming a cop—another profession that is well respected where I grew up. But a priest and a cop in one family? Now that's power and privilege in both heaven and on earth. My dad joked that maybe he would be a detective one day, just to one-up his brother. He told her that he really enjoyed his classes at John Jay, that he thought he would enjoy learning how to ski and since she was so good at it herself, maybe she would teach him some day. He then asked her if she would like to see a movie with him or grab some dinner, or maybe even both, the next weekend.

Finally, she could tell Annie she had bagged the elusive date, and there was plenty of time to see where this led before she had to think about the prom. Not that attending the prom was one of her greatest missions in life, unlike many of her classmates going into their senior year. Actually, she knew plenty of girls whose real goal was to get a ring and be walking down the church aisle shortly after they marched down the aisle on the school's football field at graduation. For many young women, even at that time, a marriage license in hand was worth more than a diploma tied with a gold ribbon. My mom had bigger plans. She wanted to work after graduation—preferably in a corporate environment, and definitely in the city. Less than fifteen miles across the river, Manhattan, or "the city" as outer-borough residents call it, was a symbol of the big time, and working there meant that you were a serious career woman making serious money, and Mom wanted her slice of that Big Apple pie.

Saturday night finally came. This was her chance to get all dolled up and be seen with a twenty-year-old college boy who was a future cop to boot. Mom's mother, Nanni, stood by smiling with pride at how beautiful my mom looked. My dad came dressed to impress, politely shook my grandfather's hand, and complimented Mom on her outfit. This scored him points—and she gave him extra points for driving from Brooklyn to Queens, only to take her back to Brooklyn to Sheepshead Bay where they were to go to Jean's for Italian food, and then catch the later showing of *Apocalypse Now.*

His car turned out to be a wreck of an old brown sedan. He opened the passenger door, but before Mom could get in, my dad slid in first, scooted over the console, and landed in the driver's seat.

He grinned as he patted the empty bucket seat to indicate she should join him. "When I first bought this hot rod the driver's side door opened just fine. Within a month it was opening only on Mondays, Wednesdays, and Fridays. Then one Friday night, it just decided to completely quit."

Mom said that she burst out laughing. She loved that he could laugh at himself. He was certainly embarrassed by the state of the car, but was creative enough to know how to turn a liability into something completely endearing. She thought that Annie was right. A date with Ray Sheehan had been worth the wait.

They drove westbound on the Belt Parkway to Emmons Avenue, where the humble restaurant awaited. Once there he did all the right things: pulled out her chair, stood when she excused herself, and picked up the check. Jean's was a great choice, as it was the kind of comfortable, neighborhood standby that could loosen up any nervous couple. They had fun talking about their interests over shrimp scampi and steak pizzaiola. By the time they got to the movie theater, Mom was feeling confident that they would see each other again. Sure enough, after he parked the car in front of her house, he asked her for a second date. After his peck on her cheek and date number two lined up, she didn't mind that she had to open the passenger door herself.

New Yorkers love food—all kinds of food, but there are three standbys that qualify for beloved staples: Italian, Chinese, and diner food. Since they had already had Italian and everyone knew that diner food was reserved for Disco Fries (steak fries covered with melted mozzarella cheese and brown gravy) after dancing into the wee hours at your favorite disco club, the obvious choice for their second date was Chinese food. This time they would stay close to Mom's home in Howard Beach. After all, school had just started and it was a weeknight.

Their conversation outlasted the speedy service of the three-course Chinese meal. Over wonton soup, they discovered a shared passion for family, agreeing that family is sacrosanct and should always come first. During shrimp lo Mein and sweet and sour chicken made for two, they agreed that a career is important, but a woman really should stay home with her children. By the time they cracked open their fortune cookies, they were deep into a discussion about their Catholic faith and the beliefs they both held dear: Church every Sunday, never eat meat on Fridays, never receive Holy Communion if you haven't gone to confession, and never believe what you read in a fortune cookie.

Everything about him made my mom feel comfortable and

safe. Predictable. She found herself thinking that she might just take him to the prom.

It was at about this point when Dad said he really wanted to date her more, and it bothered him that he couldn't since he was starting a security job. Mom said she was touched by this.

"We'll manage. It will be cool."

And that's when he said, "Hey, you should give me a call tomorrow from school."

The way he said it sounded more like an expectation than a request, and she didn't know how to respond. "From school? Why don't I just call you when I get home?"

Dad didn't seem to like her answer, or at least he wasn't going to accept it and leave it at that. What was she doing in school that was so important that she couldn't find a few minutes to give him a call during her free period?

"All seniors have free periods, Babe."

Mom said she was so thrilled that he called her Babe that she missed the red flag.

Unlike many of her friends, Mom was the type of student who never minded when September rolled around. Summer lingered through September, and coupled with the good weather was the luck of attending a high school that was situated right on the water. She went to school at Beach Channel in Rockaway, a beach-front town that bordered her hometown of Howard Beach. It was exciting to be a senior, and yet a little scary to sit on the precipice of such a life-altering event as graduation. She welcomed the ritual of making plans with her friends before first period about where they would hang out after school. It gave them something to look forward to all the way through seventh period. Notes would be passed through the halls as locations changed, but one thing was certain: they would gather somewhere. Most of the time it was at the McDonald's on the corner, but it could be at their second favorite hangout, the beach nearby.

However, the day after my dad called her Babe and sealed it with another peck on the cheek, she stopped at the phone booth outside the school building doors. When Annie wanted to know what the holdup was, she shrugged. "I need to call Ray. Just a quick call, that's all."

Annie and her other girlfriends had been teasing her with singsong taunts like "Ooh, high school boys aren't good enough for Barbara anymore." or "Barbara only dates college boys." However, Mom knew they thought it was fun and exciting, and it gave them all something to swoon over. Annie said she'd save a seat, but no promises about any leftover fries.

Mom made the call and tried to be as casual and into the conversation as much as possible while my dad played 20 Questions: What was she doing? Where was she going? Who was she going with? The questions kept coming while she yearned to join her friends and sip on a McDonald's chocolate shake. Yet she did like him and didn't want to be too hard on him for being so interested in her. That's what attracted her to him in the first place—he had a genuine interest in *her,* so of course that meant an interest in her whereabouts, friends, and social calendar.

Still, she said she was glad when the phone call ended so she could meet up with Annie and the gang. These were the pals she could count on; the girlfriends she could talk to and laugh with when they weren't flirting with boys in the various parking lots and beach lots around town. Although they did seem immature compared with her conversations with my father, she felt that it never hurt to practice up on one's flirting skills—especially since she had plans to work in the city once she graduated and was bound to be putting those skills to use.

"Ray called," Nanni said as Mom breezed through the front door. Before Mom could reply that she'd call him after supper, the phone rang again.

"Why didn't you return my call?" he immediately wanted to know when she answered.

"I was going to call you after I ate."

He went back to the Q&A, this time asking what she'd done between the call after school and the conversation they were now having. This call was brief, though, since he was on his break at the security job. That he would spend his precious fifteen-minute break talking to her again really pumped up her ego. Mom thought that she must be doing something right to have put such a spell on this guy, and she couldn't wait to tell Annie.

The next couple of days went by and the pattern persisted. "What's your schedule like at school? Call me during classes. It's too long to wait to hear from you till after you're out."

What at first seemed exciting was getting old fast. Mom began to feel like she was obligated to stop and check in with him. Her friend Annie thought he was getting way too demanding, especially since they weren't even officially a couple. Between the peer pressure of her friends and a growing resentment of having to always make sure she had enough dimes to feed the pay phone, Mom knew she had to tell him to back off. His calls to her house had become incessant. Sometimes he'd leave three or four messages with Nanni before dinnertime.

"Barbara, Ray called again. Are you going to call him back? You know if you don't, he'll just keep calling. And he'll probably question me on your whereabouts again. I don't like that."

There was no caller ID in those days, but when the phone rang yet again, they didn't need to guess who was on the other end of the line. Mom told me her stomach was in knots when she answered the phone. "Hello?"

"I need to see you. What are you doing this weekend? Can we go out?"

"Yes, I need to see you, too, Ray."

They made plans for dinner again—and this time she suggested a diner. Not only did Mom feel uncomfortable with his constant surveillance, but her friends were talking about it and now Nanni was upset. Mom knew what she needed to do, and it required a quick meal with a noisy atmosphere. Clearly, he wanted a more serious and committed relationship—even though he hadn't even kissed her yet, unless pecks on the cheek counted. She wasn't ready for all the checking in and answering to him. No, he was a nice enough guy who came from a nice enough family, but the time wasn't right for her and that's exactly what she told him over a cheeseburger and fries.

He took it well. He didn't try to kiss her goodnight, but he didn't exactly give up, either. The last thing he said was, "Can I call you?"

"No, Ray. I don't think so."

He called anyway. Twice. She never returned his calls.

Mom took her friend to the prom, and after graduation, she set off for Manhattan.

CHAPTER TWO

Escape to the City

"Reality is that which, when you stop believing in it,
doesn't go away."
—Phillip K. Dick

The A train into the city usually smelled like a combination of BO, burnt popcorn, and wet dog. In the summertime it was even worse. But even with that downside of commuting, Mom felt like she had arrived. She was a working girl, just as she planned, and the proof was in her pocketbook. Not exactly in the form of money (she was now making $297 biweekly as a clerk at Barclay Bank at 100 Water Street), but in the items she carried around in her purse: one plastic baggie filled with copper-colored subway tokens; a can of aerosol hairspray; her building ID card, peppermint Chiclets, Kleenex, a compact mirror; and a brownbag lunch Mondays through Thursdays so she could splurge on lunch with co-worker friends on Fridays. But the dead giveaway that she was a proud member of the rat race was a bottle of clear nail polish. Every working girl carried one because if she wanted to get places in her career, she was required to wear pantyhose beneath her hip-hugging skirt and therefore had to master the art of stopping a nylon run in its tracks so it didn't become an unsightly hole.

She didn't need any more holes—the one that had been in her heart since before she met my dad was plenty. Mom and Johnny Dee had dated back in high school, before her brief courtship with Dad in her senior year. She had never stopped missing her gorgeous, blond-haired, blue-eyed Johnny. They had been in love the way two kids who grow up together fall in love—hard and committed. Their comfort and familiarity blended with an intoxicating chemical and sensual connection that time had not been able to dilute. From the perspective of distance, Mom determined the reasons she had held on to her love for Johnny. One, it was real; two, they were each other's firsts; three, they were both punished for it.

When she brought Johnny Dee home to meet her family shortly after starting high school, everyone considered the relationship innocent, which at that time, it was. Other than the fact that he was from Ozone Park, the neighboring town to her home in Howard Beach, my grandparents seemed to accept him and stood aside to let their daughter explore this newfound interest in boys. But that interest led to a year of committed dating. Even as an adult working in Manhattan, Mom could still remember their first date: August 6, 1976. How could she ever forget it? She had plastered the date all over her notebooks from her freshman year through part of her junior year.

After my grandparents discovered what they "had done," it was over. She wasn't sure how they knew, because the whole scene went down mostly via nonverbal communication. My grandfather didn't get mad often, but when he did, he didn't have to yell. He'd turn red instead and purse his lips and motion with his fingers. This time the finger pointed to her room. "You're punished indefinitely." Nanni, standing behind him, arms crossed, silently backed up his command.

"And no phone!"

No phone? How could she warn Johnny? Mom thought this was the worst thing that could ever happen.

"And you are NEVER to see that boy again!"

This is what it feels like to die, my mother thought as she lay sobbing on her bed. Her chest felt like a hurting, empty cavity, as though someone had just reached in and torn out her heart. Rarely had she disappointed my grandparents, and this had to be the most severely she could hurt them, letting her emotions and hormones throw away all the moral principles they had drilled into her.

She was convinced that my grandfather would probably never look at her the same, yet he would be watching for the slightest sign of her sneaking around behind his back. And if he caught them? God help Johnny Dee. Mom felt that if she loved him at all, and she loved him so much it hurt, then the best way she could show that love would be to protect him, and that meant not seeing him anymore, even though they still cared deeply for each other.

Instinctively she knew what she had to do to make this wrong as right as possible. Catholics were big on martyrs, so a martyr she would be if that's what it took to keep Johnny Dee safe and try to earn back my grandparents' trust. There would be no teen-age defiance; only a combination of Catholic guilt and shame and an unspeakable loss that swirled uneasily around the fact that she had absolutely no regrets for giving up what she was expected to save for her husband.

After Johnny, plenty of other guys, like my father, came along, especially once she was making her way in the city. That meant an active dating life and an overflowing social calendar, thanks to new work friends and desk mates, like Mira.

Their desks faced each other so directly that if they looked up from their IBM Selectrics, they literally stared each other in the face. For two working girls that had more in common than not, the result was Mira doing her darnedest to find my mother a serious boyfriend after a string of dates from hell. Happily engaged herself, Mira understood that if her pal wanted four children, there was no time like the present to get serious about getting serious. If Mr. Right was out there, they needed to find him soon.

As Mom tells it, she started the search with a potential match that Mira sent her way. His name was Oscar. On the positive side, he looked nothing like the grouch on *Sesame Street,* nor did he have his disposition. As one of the personal bankers at Barclay, Oscar always coordinated the happy hours, and while he was a bit stocky, there was something cuddly about him. But dating Oscar proved futile. First, his favorite song was *This Magic Moment,* which, although a very nice song, seemed a bit effeminate and completely outdated. This was, after all, 1980, not 1960. But the killer as husband material was that Oscar would always send his food back at restaurants. How many ways are there to mess up a burger?

Then there was George. Mom knew him from the neighborhood, even though they didn't go to the same high school. Everyone around town called him Georgie to differentiate him from his father, George Sr., but Georgie wasn't much different from his dad. They both were on the short side with broad shoulders, thin waists, and dark, thick eyebrows that looked like caterpillars. In fact, Georgie even followed in his father's footsteps by working a construction job for the city. Mom liked the idea of dating a guy who was handy and had a union behind him. City jobs were stable and offered awesome pension plans. But as she told Mira, she wasn't even sure why Georgie asked her out since he went with Annette for years, and she was somewhat of a bimbette. Mom said that Mira howled as she recounted her one-and-only date with Georgie:

"So, we walked up and down Crossbay Boulevard, which runs perpendicular to both of our streets, and Georgie said, 'See those lines?' He's gesturing to the yellow double traffic lines separating the two lanes.

"The street's busy, so I figure he doesn't want me to get hurt, and all I can think to say back is, 'Yeah?'

"And Georgie says, 'I painted them.'

" 'You painted the lines?' I say.

" 'Yeah, I also did the ones on Jamaica Avenue.'

" 'Wow!' I say, trying to sound excited because he's popping his buttons he's so proud. And when he looks like he's still waiting for me to tell him how wonderful that is, the only thing I can think to say is, 'That's . . . *neat?*' I thought he was going to cry."

Shortly after that, Mom met Payton while waiting for the elevator one morning. He didn't work for the bank; he did something in insurance. He looked like a Payton—over six-feet tall, fair, and very thin with mousy brown hair parted on the left side. It was neat and plastered, like a Ken doll. Payton was definitely a step up from any of the guys she had dated before. He took her to a fancy place in SoHo for sushi, which she had never eaten in her life. She didn't even know anyone who ate sushi, or Japanese food, for that matter.

The first thing Mom noticed about the upscale restaurant was how the dining room was filled with all shapes, sizes and colors of bamboo. They reminded her of flutes, which echoed the exotic sound being piped from the ceiling. It was a really high ceiling, and the constant murmur of the posh crowd sounded like static as she kept from making eye contact with Payton until she could think of an icebreaker for the awkward moment.

Their conversation went something like this:

"I like your glasses. They remind me of Doc's on the *Love Boat.*"

"I usually wear contact lenses," he replied, ignoring the reference to one of her favorite shows, "but I woke up late today and threw them on."

"Well, they look good on you. You wear them well."

"Thanks."

"You're welcome."

When the silence lengthened from uncomfortable to downright painful, she gave it another try. "Soooo . . . I never met a person named Payton. How neat that you are named after a town!"

"Sorry?"

"You know, *Peyton Place.* The town. The show. It was my parents' favorite. When I was growing up, they'd sometimes let me and my brother and sister watch it with them, but only once in a while."

"Can't say I've seen it," Payton answered. "My parents don't watch much television. And Payton is a family name. It goes back generations. My great-great-grandfather owned a lot of land in Connecticut, but nothing in a town called Payton."

After Mom told Mira about her agonizing date with Payton, Mira suggested they break her bad luck streak by taking a vacation together to Disney World. "It will be so much fun. C'mon, Barb, a girls' getaway! Live a little. See the world."

Shortly after Mom returned from Florida, old Mrs. Campbell died. She lived around the corner from Our Lady of Grace. She spoke with an English accent and gave out toffee cookies when neighborhood kids like Mom walked by her house. Her passing was sad news, but such deaths in the community typically spark a communal event—beginning with the gathering at a funeral home to "wake" the deceased, followed by a mournful burial, and then the collective gorging at a grandiose feast. Except for the six-feet-under part, Mom said that the whole thing reminded her of any other celebration for a life-altering event, like a wedding or a christening. Or a priest's ordination.

She couldn't make the two to four viewing at the funeral parlor because she had to work, so she planned on heading over there for the seven to nine to pay her last respects. That she had neglected to dress in black that morning didn't dawn on her until she took off her coat. That's when she, and seemingly everyone around her, noticed the eye-popping, red cashmere sweater she was wearing. Soon, however, Mom noticed that she wasn't the only one attracting attention. She heard a racket that sounded like a two-way radio.

She turned to see a tall police officer fumbling with his radio and making a quick exit around the corner back into the vestibule mumbling, "*Shit, damn, shit . . .*"

He reentered the room composed, ignoring the fact that the room full of mourners had all stared him down just seconds before, as central dispatch hollered numbers and commands at a decibel that could wake the dead.

"Ray Sheehan?" Mom asked in a whisper as she kneeled next to him on the bench in front of Mrs. Campbell.

"Barbara Henry," he whispered her name back with a smile, while making the sign of the cross.

As they both bowed heads, instead of praying, Mom counted the years that had passed since she had last seen him. It amazed her that nearly three years could fly by so fast, and it reinforced her desire to get on with life. Mrs. Campbell had been young once, but one would never know it to see her withered body and wrinkled face as she lay there in the coffin. A quick glance at my dad, so vital and in control, gave her a new appreciation of the line they were straddling between maturity and youth. The years had been good to him. His once bushy hair was still thick, but shorter and tamed. His uniformed body formed a silhouette that shot down the stereotype of doughnut-eating cops.

By silent assent they found their way to a love seat at the back of the room, where Mom didn't have to pretend to be impressed. "Wow, you're a police officer!" she exclaimed and wasn't even embarrassed to have stated something so obvious. Neither did she have to feign genuine interest when she asked, "Where are you stationed?"

"The six-oh. Coney Island." His smile was even more engaging than she remembered. "Been there going on two years."

"I remember you said you wanted to be a cop. It's nice to see you made that happen."

"And what about you?" He playfully nudged her shoulder. "Are you the working girl you told me you'd become?"

"I am."

"Do you like it?"

It wasn't a question that had ever been posed to her, so she hesitated while searching for an answer. Working, especially right out of high school, provided a break in the monotony of day-to-day school life that had monopolized her routine for as long as she could remember. The big city—and all of the movies that glamorized it—seemed like a noble goal. And she did like her job enough to keep getting up at the crack of dawn to plan her outfits and make the 7:22, but she wasn't looking forward to a life of commuting and answering phones or staring Mira in the face indefinitely. The best she could come up with for an answer was sort of a cop-out.

"Yes and no," she finally decided.

"That's life. We think it's supposed to be one way and then it turns out to be something else. Better in some ways. Not so good in others." Dad nodded toward the coffin. "But looking on the bright side, anything's better than this."

Mom's stifled giggle came out as a snort, which in turn caused Dad to chuckle. It reminded her of when they first met and how funny he was. He still seemed interested in her. She wondered why she had broken up with him. Then she remembered—all the probing questions, all the phone calls. It had been as though he were policing her. But could it be that he was just practicing the profession that suited him so well? Mom wanted to think so. She wanted to come up with some logical reason for what had been some pretty irrational behavior, because she liked the way he made her laugh, liked the way he understood the community they had both grown up in, and that he wasn't some snotty heir to half of Connecticut and his public service went beyond painting asphalt. He had never embarrassed her in a restaurant, and he was Catholic, too. Could it be that she had misjudged him somehow? After all, she had only been a senior in high school and was still nursing a broken heart. And so the rationalizing began that was to be such a detrimental part of Mom's life over the next twenty-four years.

Dad suddenly shook his head, and immediately his posture, voice, and expression all shifted from light to somber, and she had to wonder if he could read minds.

"You must have thought I was out of line when you broke up with me. And I'm really sorry for that, Barbara. I think in my own way I was trying to show interest, but I see how I came too fast out of the gate. Guns blazing, if you know what I mean," he added, doing his best John Wayne impression.

Mom wondered if he were asking her for a second chance. If so, would she be dumb enough to go there again? Or dumb not to? After all, she had probably been comparing my dad to Johnny, and no one could have lived up to him. Now that she knew there were a lot more frogs out there than princes, dating a cop did have its appeal, especially when the cop was sensitive to her perception of

their past, man enough to bring it up, and sincere enough to actually apologize for it.

Dad's radio went off again.

"Whoa! That sounds serious!" Mom said.

The static in the background broke the moment and his mood
shifted once again, this time to official business.

"I'm on my meal, so I have to keep my radio on."

Teasing him, she said, "Is that the same thing as a dinner
break?"

"Yeah, you know . . . us cops have a lingo for everything."

"Ten-four, good buddy!"

"Not *exactly* the *Dukes of Hazzard,* but I guess you're close
enough," Dad teased back, and she liked the easy banter, liked how
he tipped his hat and said, "I guess I can make you an honorary
cop."

The way he fidgeted with his badge like he might take it off
and put it on her made her think that he was flirting.

"You like that show, too?" she asked eagerly.

"Yeah, I love lots of TV."

"Me too."

And so it went. As they bonded over the *Dukes of Hazzard*
within sight of Mrs. Campbell's corpse, Mom had to wonder at the
irony of it all.

Reunited over death, she thought she had found what had been
missing in life.

CHAPTER THREE

Denial

"Hope is the denial of reality."
—MARGARET WEIS

Raymond and I weren't very close to our grandparents on our dad's side, so hearing about them from Mom was interesting—and it explained a lot about my dad. However, it didn't excuse what he chose to be. Both of his parents are now deceased. It is a blessing that they didn't see what their son had become.

The first time my dad took my mom home to meet his parents, his mother, Edith, was waving a broom at the next-door neighbor, and not in a good way. She was one of those ladies who liked to sweep water along street gutters with a stiff straw-bristled broom. Italian ladies, at least the ones Mom knew growing up, did this on a daily basis; they also enjoyed spraying down the sidewalk with a hose for no reason at all. Mom would soon learn that from the first sign of spring to the first snowfall, Grandma Edith was in the ranks of those who considered it their right and duty to perform cement-watering chores while imploring random people in a thick Brook-lyn accent to "shut up your kids" or "stay away from my house."

But it wasn't *her* house, as it turned out, and Mom reasoned maybe that's why she seemed so angry. My dad's family rented the one-bedroom cape in the Bensonhurst section of Brooklyn from one of Grandma Edith's nephews. He couldn't have been charging them much rent, because my grandma didn't work and my grand-father didn't have a high-paying job. According to what my father told my mom, my grandfather had worked at a print shop for a while, but that was when he still had fingers and could work the press. She never fully understood what happened, but it had some-thing to do with a machine accident—maybe in the printing shop. Now he had just one thumb on his right hand, which left him dis-abled when it came to manual labor, and that was about all he was trained for, except for some security work he did once in a while.

She said that my grandfather didn't really say much. He usu-ally kept to himself in his small living room that was purposely kept dark, firmly planted in a chair that reminded Mom of the one that Archie Bunker sat in, although he wasn't ornery like Mr. Bunker, and he wasn't racist. Mom said that my grandfather seemed sad, even when everyone left him alone—the way he liked it—to watch his sports and eat his food.

This first visit, however, was pretty much kept out of the TV room and closer to the kitchen.

"She staying for dinner?" Grandma Edith asked my dad, ges-turing to Mom as if she were a stray cat he had just rescued from the street.

"Sure, Ma. She'll stay."

Mom wasn't used to being spoken about like she wasn't in the room, and she wasn't very hungry despite my dad having sworn up and down that his mother's cooking was something out of heaven. Unfortunately, unless she wanted to be even ruder than my grandma, she felt that she had no choice but to stay for dinner.

Mom said they had been officially boyfriend and girlfriend for only a few weeks, so as they took their places around the orange Formica dinner table, the "meet the parents" moment was uncomfortable. Mom wished it were taking place at a more public event, with other people around to relieve the pressure. Given their surprising lack of sociability in their own house, she wondered how they could have turned out such personable sons. Not just my dad and Danny, but Dad's twin brother Vincent who gave Mom several encouraging smiles during an unexpectedly tense conversation at the dinner table that went something like this:

"Did you see the Martinelli's new car next door?" Grandma Edith directed the remark to no one in particular. "It's junk. And it takes too much room in the driveway. Stupid."

My dad said, "Yeah, Ma, but it's a nice car, and it's not bothering nobody."

"Don't talk back! You're not too bright, talking to your mother like that."

She glared directly at him until he shifted his dark eyes down to his bowl of beans and pasta. Her mouth formed the shape of an upside-down horseshoe, as if magnets were pulling it down from either side—permanently.

She then shook her finger at my dad. "Them, and the other ones around the corner, they're no better. They think they are better than me, with their fancy new fence and swimming pool? *Pah.*" It was a question not meant to be answered.

Throughout dinner, the rant continued, and she did a decent job of convincing herself that she was not inferior to the people down the block or around the corner or up the street, who were all doing things, buying things, being things that she obviously was not.

Mom managed to get a few swallows of pasta past the tightness in her throat as she worried that my dad would speak up again. She was grateful when he didn't say anything. Nobody did.

Once inside the car and headed home, Mom couldn't restrain her groan of relief

"Oh, c'mon, it wasn't that bad, Barb," my dad tried to reassure her. "Besides, I think they liked you."

"Like me? Are you kidding? Did you see how your mom looked at you when she asked if I was staying for dinner—like I was some stray cat and she doesn't like cats?"

"She's like that with everyone. Don't pay any attention. The movie will make you forget all about it." Then he took a deep breath and rushed his words, as if he wanted to get them out before changing his mind. "It's funny, though, that you bring that up about stray cats. You're right, my mom, she doesn't like them and . . . well, maybe I got that from her because I used to do this funny thing to cats in the neighborhood when I was little."

"What do you mean?"

"I called it the kitty kite."

Mom said that the way he shifted in the driver's seat as he drove suggested that he was more nervous than proud to unburden this piece of personal history, and after experiencing that stressful dinner, Mom felt her heart soften. Growing up in that household could not have been easy, and whatever she was about to hear couldn't be half as bad as being raised by someone who seemed to be so mean-spirited. How that hadn't been passed on to her three fine sons, she didn't know, but she was glad that my dad felt safe enough with her to confess whatever he was about to confess as they turned the corner into the theater parking lot. Once there she prompted him to explain, "Now just what exactly is a kitty kite?"

"Okay, believe it or not, here goes. See, nobody could control the damn stray cat problem we had in the neighborhood. Even the dicks over at pest control wouldn't handle the problem, so I took matters into my own hands, right? I bought balloons and filled them up with helium . . . I'm talking *real fat* balloons, and I tied them to a string and then I'd grab the little fuckers and tie the balloons to them—a kitty kite—and then the balloon would lift them into the air and they'd be meowing and stuff and they'd float over the house and away, till we didn't have a cat infestation anymore. I was just doing my civic duty, you know?"

Mom wasn't sure whether to be appalled or give into the laughter that was bubbling up from the cartoon visual. Surely he was joking, which would be just like him to want to give her a laugh after enduring such a grim evening.

"You're putting me on! I don't believe, you!" She noticed that he hadn't joined her in the laugh-fest, but he did have a sheepish grin on his face. Just to reassure herself that it was because he had pulled a fast one and not because, God forbid, the story was actually true and he found it amusing, she challenged his claim. "I don't even think that's physically possible."

"Well, I guess that's for me to know and for you to find out."

Mom had trouble following the movie. She wasn't sure if it was because she was emotionally exhausted from meeting the Sheehans or if it had more to do with the kitty kite story. She couldn't help but wonder that even if the story weren't true, and it just couldn't be, what kind of mind could think up such a thing? He apparently had a sick sense of humor that could come out once you really got to know him, but who was she to judge him for that? He had made her laugh, which wasn't any different from comedians like Richard Pryor who told off-color jokes, and it wasn't exactly like a moral failing or something. That particular piece of guilt belonged to her. She still hadn't told him about Johnny Dee and she knew why. There was a good chance that he would break up with her once he knew she wasn't a virgin.

Mom said she realized how preposterous that would seem now, or even to Mira and many other young women her age at that time. But there were still young people like her and my dad who had been raised on certain religious principles—like the ones that she and Johnny Dee broke up over, with her playing the martyr and not having the nerve to defy my grandparents. So with the Catholic thing and the fact that he had a priest for a brother who had taken a vow of chastity, it was a pretty safe bet that he wouldn't find her desirable after she told him she hadn't saved herself. Mom thought if she didn't make a big deal out of the kitty kite thing, which was something that my dad seemed to be ashamed of, he would appreciate it and remember that when she told him about Johnny Dee—and she would have to tell him once things progressed to a more intimate level.

Intimacy was a slow progression—as in nonexistent. After a few months of dating, Mom began to have some self-esteem issues about her desirability. Not only that, but she was beginning to fear for her safety every time they got into the car. My dad's driving had become increasingly aggressive and it was scaring her. She thought some of the driving techniques he was practicing were maneuvers he might have learned at the police academy, but she couldn't believe the officers were taught how to taunt other drivers on the road, either on duty or off.

It took her a while to work up the nerve to confront him about this. She couldn't say why she was so hesitant since she had no problem speaking up for herself if someone was being a jerk on the subway or a retail clerk copped a superior attitude at the cosmetics counter. No, it was with authority figures such as parents, clergy and employers that she had difficulty asserting herself. Since my dad was her boyfriend and none of the above, the cause for her hesitation was truly a mystery to her.

Then one night they were on the Belt Parkway heading back to her house after an evening out with one of Dad's police buddies and his wife, when a black Toyota Supra changed lanes without signaling.

"Look at this fucking douche bag!" he yelled, flinging his right hand in the direction of the small sports car. Mom's head snapped backward as he slammed his foot on the accelerator. "I can't believe he just cut me off!"

"He didn't cut you off! Please," she pleaded. "Slow down!"

"Mind your business. You don't know jack shit."

My mom was still reeling from the words that felt like a slap when he swerved the car into the right lane and then accelerated until their position became even with the unsuspecting Supra driver. Then he hit the horn and didn't let off.

"Hey, asshole! Asshole! Yeah, you! What the fuck? Where's your signal! You almost killed us!"

Thankfully, the Supra driver wasn't looking for any trouble and slowed down until all they could see were the Supra's headlights in the rearview mirror. He continued flipping the driver the bird while shouting more obscenities into the rearview mirror, and honking the horn feverishly.

"Stop the car. I want to get out," she said with a sense of calm that surprised her. She felt as if she had just survived a near-death experience and nothing had the power to frighten her as much again.

"What's with the drama, Barb? People can't just not signal on the road. They're bound to kill someone."

"You almost killed *us*!" She slapped the dashboard in frustration for what he had just done, and for his ugly insinuation that she was stupid. "You think I don't know jack? Well I know this— being all crazy and not watching what's in front of you is bound to kill us *and* someone else."

"Watch your mouth. Know your place. It's my job to watch for assholes on the road. Don't *you* tell *me* my job."

Mom was ready to come right back at him when she saw the JFK Airport exit sign and knew she would be home in a few minutes. All she wanted was to get home safely; then she would let him know her feelings with a slam of the car door and not so much as a "good night." Which is exactly what she did.

For nearly a week, she refused to take his calls at home and at work. She punished him with her silence and did some serious thinking. Did she really want to stay in this relationship? Were the good times and great laughs they had worth the trade-off of his apparent lack of desire for her, his vicious outburst and the disrespectful way he spoke to her, not unlike the way his mother spoke to him?

She wished she hadn't thought about his mother at that moment, because whenever she was around my Grandma Edith, her heart went out to my dad; to his brothers and his father also, but mostly to him, because he was the only one who dared to pipe up from time to time in someone else's defense, even knowing that ridicule would be his reward. The awful first dinner had turned into several equally awful encounters. If anything, grandma's meanness seemed to escalate.

Mom marveled at how the men in the family dealt with it in their own way without striking back: there was my grandfather working the remote control with his lone thumb; there was Danny doing such good in the community, perhaps spending all his time at the parish to avoid what was anything but heaven at home; there was Vincent, who simply smiled through it all and didn't make waves; and then there was my dad, the jokester of the group who made up silly stories about floating kitties and worked like a dog but never complained. He had such passion for his work. Worthy work, too, keeping the community he loved safe. She wondered if he loved her even a little bit as much. He hadn't said he loved her, and he sure hadn't talked or acted like it during his road rage incident, but there was something inside her that hoped he did. The fact of the matter was, she missed him. She wished she didn't, but she did. And when a letter appeared in the mailbox, addressed to her with the Sheehan's return address, she couldn't wait to rip open the baby blue envelope.

She giggled at the picture of the fuzzy gray kitten with crystal blue eyes that graced the cover of the card, and at the idea of how ridiculous she had been for worrying that his crazy kitty-kite story might actually be true. With that, she opened the card.

It was blank inside except for his prose, which in his neatest handwriting said:

I may not be perfect, but you make me want to try to be.
I love you and I'm sorry. So stop punishing me.
Please answer the phone soon.

Love, Ray

Probably the last thing a person wants to hear about is details of her parents' intimate dating moments; and most likely, the last thing a mother wants to share with her daughter and son. I asked my mom about all aspects of her relationship with my father because I felt there would have been signs along the way that something wasn't right, and there were—many. Again, my hope is that if you recognize some danger signs in your own relationship as you read this book, perhaps my sharing these details will help you end it before it is too late.

If the best part of breaking up was making up, Mom wanted some proof positive evidence of that truth. After the card and the poem, she couldn't resist giving him a call. He sounded relieved to hear her voice, and after apologies were exchanged, she felt that they had reached a relationship milestone—they'd had their first official fight and were adult enough to let it go. For better or for worse, at least so far, she figured they must be falling in love since the threat of breaking up made the two of them realize how much they wanted to be together.

She told my dad that she wanted some quiet time with him, so they made plans to order in and watch television in my grandparents' basement. When he showed up with daisies and a palm-sized Ziggy doll holding a daisy of its own, she knew this was the night they would finally do the whole "kiss and make up" routine.

The idea of getting even a little physical stole her appetite. She couldn't eat more than half a bowl of wonton soup. She wanted to kiss him, but not the way they had been kissing for the last three months. They were often surrounded by friends, siblings, or parents, but when they were alone in the car . . . well, he was probably just showing respect to a nice girl, that's all. Besides, he didn't know her secret about Johnny Dee, and she had never behaved aggressively or tried to instigate a hot and heavy make-out session herself.

She felt that maybe things were about to change. They had made up from their first official fight but there was no kissing, no hugging, no affection. Mom wasn't used to that. Although Johnny Dee was her first true love, she had many dates with different guys. They all made her feel desirable and although she was a good catholic girl, she liked the attention she received. My dad didn't give that to her—he didn't make her feel special. She decided that she could still be a nice girl, but fudge the rules.

Locking her arms around his neck, she took the lead and began to kiss him like he had never kissed her before. He kissed her back, but it was sloppy. This was nothing like Johnny Dee or any of the other guys mom had dated.

"I'm not comfortable," he said as he jerked away from her.

My mom thought this had come so naturally with Johnny Dee. "What's wrong?"

"What has gotten into you, Barbara? I thought you were a nice girl."

He shoved her aside, rushed across the room, and wedged himself in the far corner of the basement. He just stood there, facing the wall with his head lowered like a Catholic schoolboy punished by his teacher for shooting spitballs or something. It looked like he was fiddling with his zipper, but that made no sense. She felt not only rejected, but also gross and tainted.

"I *am* a nice girl!" She was desperate to defend herself and just as desperate to keep her voice from carrying upstairs where my grandparents were. "Ray, look at me! There are so many people that think I'm desirable, what is wrong with you?"

She was talking to the wall, literally, as he continued to face the corner and do whatever he was doing in the region of his crotch. When he responded, his voice was strained, a little choppy, and harsh. "Maybe my mother is right and you are not the marrying type."

A lump lodged in my mom's throat. Was this going to be the time and place to tell him her secret? It didn't seem opportune at all, but they couldn't have a future with this between them—especially since it seemed obvious that this twenty-four-year-old police officer had never been with a woman before and he didn't know how to react.

She began sobbing and couldn't stop. She wasn't sure what had triggered such an emotional reaction—the fact that he had inadvertently let on that he was thinking about marrying her and she'd probably botched it up, or the fact that he wasn't Johnny. The thought that her tears were commemorating a love she hadn't felt since high school caused her to cry even harder.

My father finally turned from the wall and he hugged her to him tightly and said with such remorse that she thought it had to be genuine, "Don't cry, Barbara. I'm so sorry. I didn't mean it."

"You are disgusted by me." She said it like the accusation it was between breathy hiccups. "You said you loved me, but you don't. Go ahead, admit it."

"God! No, I was just—I don't know what made me say those things. It's just the way I was raised or something so I reacted without thinking. I didn't mean a word, I swear. I think you're amazing. Don't you know that? I wouldn't be here if I didn't think you were."

"How can you expect me to ever believe that, after you just said I'm not the kind of girl a man wants to marry?" She couldn't look him in the eyes.

"Hey, look at me. Chin up." He crooked a finger beneath her chin, directing her teary gaze to his. His eyes were warm now, no longer accusing and cold; and when his hands covered hers they were warm and gentle. Yet she was astounded when he said, "My ma was wrong. What says 'you *are* the marrying type' better than 'let's get married?'"

CHAPTER FOUR

The Engagement

"Where we have strong emotions,
we're liable to fool ourselves."
—CARL SAGAN

The few weeks following my dad's impromptu apology/proposal passed without fanfare, and Mom's emotional commitment to the idea of getting married was tenuous. Dad hadn't gotten down on bended knee as she had played out in her head, and she still hadn't received a ring, so she wasn't comfortable with telling her girlfriends that she was engaged. But one Saturday morning that all changed. Dad called and told her to bring my grandparents along for the big event that would take place at his family's home the next day. The jeweler that my dad's family had always done business with for special occasions was coming to their house to show the soon-to-be bride and groom some engagement rings. Mom was excited about the idea of the jeweler making house calls—very much like family physicians once did. In the car on the way to her future in-laws' house, Nanni congratulated her for the first time, although with a hint at the perils that came with rushing to the altar. "It's a little fast to decide to spend the rest of your life with someone after just a little over three months of dating . . . but Ray's a good catch."

Mom latched on to that last part, because she sincerely cared what my grandparents thought. Marrying my dad was logical, even if she was a little shaky about the love part of it. And he *was* a good catch, just as Nanni had said. He had an upstanding job and came from a good Catholic family. Even if his mother was not someone she would have chosen for a mother-in-law, Grandma Edith had given birth to a priest, plus two other fine sons. Mom said she prayed that my grandma wouldn't embarrass her or my dad on this special day; that she wouldn't say or do something to give her mother cause to take back the much needed affirmation that "Yes, this is a good thing."

"He's a hard worker," Mom was quick to say after Nanni's comment. She wanted to shore up this opinion—pile on enough positives to get the nod of approval she hadn't yet received from my grandfather. "He'll be taking the sergeant's exam soon enough and then he'll do whatever it takes to become a detective. I'm sure he can do it."

She *was* sure because even if my dad wasn't Mr. Perfect, and a girl could wait forever if she was holding out for such a man, she did know that he was intelligent, resourceful, ambitious, and would make a good provider. When she said as much, my grandfather slowly nodded and gave her a little smile. It was enough to let my mom know that he wasn't holding a grudge, since the one customary act of respect he was entitled to—having a man ask for his daughter's hand in marriage—was not going to happen. My dad wasn't someone who felt obligated to conform to certain traditional customs. However, having my grandparents present to witness the selection of the wedding jewelry must count for something, because Mom noticed they exchanged a glance that looked more hopeful than resigned.

When they arrived at Dad's house, Mr. Levine, the jeweler, was already there, and Mom's relief was immense when Grandma Edith cordially offered everyone bagels and cream cheese, along with the coffee she had brewing in the cast iron pot on the stovetop. The steaming coffee created a warm atmosphere, and it smelled wonderful. Mom thought that my dad smelled good too, as he gave her a perfunctory kiss on the cheek.

Mr. Levine, an older gentleman who had a storefront on Flatbush Avenue, burst forth with the kind of enthusiastic congratulations that made this the magic moment Mom had been waiting for. She said that judging from the way Dad beamed at her, he had been waiting for this moment as well.

However, the moment didn't last long. In her usual gruff manner, Grandma Edith abruptly told everyone to sit down. My mom knew by this time to follow suit with my dad and simply do as "requested," whereas those unacquainted with her abrasiveness weren't prepared for it any more than my mom was the first time she had dinner at my dad's house.

Mom had not told anyone in her family about that particular incident or the ones that followed because she didn't want my dad to be unfairly judged by the ill conduct of his mother. Just as my mom had done that first night at dinner, everyone did as they were told—their good manners too ingrained to question the hostess in her own kitchen.

They all took their filled cups to the seats Grandma Edith assigned around the rectangular Formica table. She nudged Mr. Levine toward the middle of the table, where he was to be flanked by my parents. Mr. Sheehan was appointed to stand at the head, my grandparents relegated across from my parents, and then Grandma Edith took her place, standing over my dad's shoulder.

"Barbara, do you see anything you like?" The tone of the question from my grandma was harsh. Mom said that strangely enough it didn't disturb her too much since she had grown somewhat accustomed to her "way with words." What disturbed her were the stunned expressions on my grandparents' faces when she added, "Even though there are not many choices for you."

"Excuse me?" Mom said what she knew Nanni must have been thinking.

"You're not gonna walk out of here with Elizabeth Taylor's rock on your finger. Isn't that right, Ray?"

My mom didn't know if Grandma Edith intended to humiliate my dad or protect his pocketbook—or maybe both. Mom told me that that was the weird thing about my dad's mom. In her own way, she seemed to care about the welfare of her children, but didn't show it like Mom was accustomed to. Maybe that's why she felt the need to give her the benefit of the doubt.

"I don't want anything crazy," Mom assured Mr. Levine, hoping that my dad would get the message too. "I'm okay with whatever Ray can afford."

"What am I, some kind of deadbeat? Of course I can afford whatever you want. Go ahead, take your pick."

"Ray, really, it's okay."

"Listen to her, Ray. She'll be just as happy with the smallest ring in the case."

"Ma, enough!" Dad shouted.

If there was a tipping point of tolerance, he had clearly reached his with his mother. The last time my mom had seen him so angry was during his road rage incident on the Belt Parkway.

"I have small hands, Mrs. Sheehan, so how thoughtful of you to notice how gaudy a big ring would look." Determined to move things along so she could get herself and my grandparents out of there as soon as possible, Mom pointed to the low-set marquis-shaped diamond in a gold band, which was far from the most expensive selection in the box but clearly deemed "out of the price range," judging by the loud sigh coming from Grandma Edith. To her credit, she limited her disapproval to the sigh and not words.

"Without hesitation, Dad pulled the ring from the slit it sat in." This one," he said.

"Great. It's beautiful. Thank you, Ray," Mom said.

And with that my dad slipped the ring on as if it were made for her finger.

By the time my dad picked up the ring from Mr. Levine, Mom was bursting to be a bride. The first person she wanted to show her ring to was Annie, who was already engaged to a plumber named Paul and was planning a wedding to end all weddings at the Coral House on Long Island. Paul proposed to Annie with a fortune cookie after dinner at a Chinese restaurant. When Annie cracked open her cookie to find a ring, Paul got down on bended knee in front of about twenty people and formally proposed with the flashy carat-and-a-half marquis-cut raised diamond that had to have cost a bundle.

Paul was the type of guy who trusted strangers, and my dad was a skeptical cop conditioned to expect the very worst from people, but despite these differences, he and Paul got along pretty well. This was a relief to Mom, because she and Annie had vowed to be best friends forever. Mom thought now that my dad and Paul were friends, they could have weekly couples' nights, take getaway vacations together, and go on exhaustingly wonderful trips to Disney World with their future kids, who would be best friends too.

"We have to celebrate!" Annie exclaimed. "You guys should come skiing with us. Paul and I keep saying we want to go to the Poconos for the weekend while we still have some good snow, and this is the perfect excuse. It will be so much fun!"

Mom enthusiastically agreed but quickly realized there might be a glitch because Dad didn't know how to ski. Also—if this entailed a sleepover, that could be a problem. Annie and Paul would definitely plan to share a bed, but Dad wouldn't be comfortable doing the same with her. So Mom hedged by saying, "I'll find out Ray's work schedule and let you know. He's been working a lot."

Annie knew what it was like dating a man who worked a lot. Paul had a great job as a plumber and was determined to work his way to his own business. Similarly, my dad knew exactly the track he needed to take to make sergeant, and he was paying his dues by taking prep classes and studying for the six-hour mandatory exam. He also picked up a lot of overtime to help save enough for a honeymoon in Hawaii, which was the same place Annie and Paul were going for their honeymoon. Mom didn't see the point of spending so much money on a trip when there were plenty of less expensive options, but when Paul told my dad that he and Annie had booked a five-star resort in Maui, Dad said they would be doing the same. Mom told me that he had not discussed this with her, and she really didn't know much about Maui except that it took eleven hours on a plane to get there and was five time zones away, both of which made her feel a little out of her comfort zone. But it seemed to please my dad that they, too, would have a lavish honeymoon. She liked to see him happy so she didn't protest.

Neither did he balk for a second at the idea of going to the Poconos. He leaped at the chance to take on the challenge of learning to ski. Mom was pleased because he played softball in the NYPD league, and she loved cheering him on from the bleachers with the other girlfriends and wives of his buddies. She thrived on the socialization and sense of belonging to yet another community, just as my dad was excited about this skiing trip with Annie and Paul. It seemed to Mom at the time that they had their act together and really were well matched, even though Dad suggested they take a separate car from Annie and Paul so they could make the two-hour drive back that Saturday evening rather than stay overnight and make it a full weekend.

My mom couldn't remember when she'd had so much fun, and a lot of that had to do with Dad's being such a good sport on the slopes. She said he tackled them with all the finesse of Frankenstein's dancing a waltz. Mom enjoyed playing instructor and gave him his first pointers in the snowplow, the traditional stance for beginners.

"Okay, I'm ready now. I got this," he said confidently after one turn down the bunny slope. "Let's hit the lift! This slope is mine!"

Mom was concerned. "But, Ray, don't you want to take a real lesson first? You really need to learn how to slow down better. You keep crossing your skis, and I don't think you'll want the little ski ambulance making a rescue run for your broken body."

Dad had that stubborn expression on his face that she had come to think of as an unstoppable force meeting an unmovable object. It was one of those traits that fall into an odd dichotomy; the things you admire about a person are also the part of their personality that drives you nuts. Yes, he did confuse her sometimes with his contradictory behaviors, but that was part of what made him so interesting to her. Besides, she told herself, she had a lifetime of marriage to figure him out and she thought that was a good thing.

"I'm not taking lessons with a bunch of six-year-olds," he asserted with a stab of his poles into the snow. He then did his mood switch and poured on the charm. "Plus, it looks like such a romantic ride to the top and with you by my side, how can I possibly fall . . . except more in love?"

Mom said that my dad didn't usually swoon over her or whisper sweet nothings in her ear, but when he did come out with something romantic, he was smooth—and irresistible.

As the chair lifted them slowly to the top of the mountain, Mom knew sheer bliss as she watched him swing his legs in midair like a carefree child on a playground swing. They held hands and watched each other exhale steamy puffs of breath—until she realized that she had forgotten one of the most important lessons of all.

"Once you get to the top, you need to push off the chair with your butt," she explained. "And you have to be quick, or else the chair will whack you right in the head. Got it?"

"Being on my toes is what I do for a living."

"Then get your poles ready . . . and . . . go!"

The chair dipped out from under her, and she planted both feet and poles at the landing. When she turned around there was my dad, lying on the ground with one shin tucked beneath him and his other leg sprawled to his left side. But he had managed to keep his gloved hands gripped to each pole.

"Ray! Are you all right?" The urgency in her voice was replaced with a great big laugh when she saw him grinning. "You look like one of those crime scene silhouettes!" she teased while my dad just lay there, playing dead. In that moment she couldn't bear the thought of his dying; her life would be colorless without his jokes and solid presence as they faced the world together. Seeing him vulnerable like this, and so teddy bear-adorable, it was hard to believe this was the same man who had gone berserk in the car and had called her bad names in my grandparents' basement.

It took him a while, but once he got to his feet and looked down the slope, he blew out a whistle and said, "How the hell am I supposed to get down there from up here?"

"Ray, there's only one way down this slope. Just remember—snowplow!"

Fueled by the endorphins from laughing so hard, off she went, only for Dad to pass her by. As he picked up more and more speed, Mom screamed from behind him, "Snowplow! Snowplow!" He went around the bend and plowed all right—straight into an older man, whom he hit so hard, the man's red hat flew off.

When he did finally get to the bottom, his inevitable fall was first broken by a group of novice skiers taking the beginner's ski class, and then a tree. Covered in pine needles and snow, he looked up at the instructor and said plainly, "Maybe I should join your class."

Everyone clapped, and Mom knew that she would marry him right then and there if a priest were making the rounds on skis.

Hindsight is so clear, but it wasn't that clear at the time Mom was living it. There were signs of abuse even in the dating/engagement period. My dad obviously had issues—the way he drove, controlling her every move, calling her all the time, making her report in—the signs were all there; even the manipulation when he thought she was getting away, which although it seemed endearing to her at the time, was a sign of abuse.

Annie and Paul's wedding was in the spring—April of 1983. Monstrous cameras flashed at Annie's house that morning, while wedding photographers and videographers captured each precious moment of her preparations as if she were a leading lady. In the supporting role, Mom played the maid of honor. The excitement of the day further ignited her anticipation of how her own wedding day would play out in early October. They chose that month because it was one of her favorite times of year. They could still count on some beautiful weather as well as use the warm autumn themes and colors.

She and Dad met up at the reception hall after the hour-long church ceremony. It was the first time he'd seen her formally dressed up, with her hair pulled back in a French twist and makeup professionally applied.

"Wow, look at you!" He seemed genuinely surprised by her appearance, which made her wonder if he might find her more desirable if she dolled herself up more often. After all, they still hadn't gone beyond chaste kisses since that disastrous night when she'd put the moves on him in the basement. "Are you wearing red lipstick?"

"Yeah, the makeup lady said blondes wear red lipstick well, so I said what the hell?" She wanted him to tell her he thought she was beautiful. She had heard that from other guys she had dated, but never from my dad. In fact, the first time she heard it was a very long time ago, and it was Johnny Dee who had said it. She wanted my dad's voice to dilute the echo from her past—wanted to hear the word "beautiful" from the man who was going to become her husband in less than six months.

She didn't hear the words, but she contented herself with the squeeze of his hand under the table as they sat at the dais with the rest of the bridal party, all eyes on Annie and Paul as Paul's best man gave the toast and glasses were tapped with silverware to urge another kiss.

"You guys are next," said Susan, another friend and fellow bridesmaid. Susan was married to Terry and was always looking forward to another one of her friends joining the club, or as Terry jokingly called it, "biting the dust."

"That's right, and it's really official now that I bought Barbara her engagement ring." He grabbed her hand to show Susan and Terry her left ring finger.

"I know, it's absolutely beautiful," Susan replied graciously.

"Yeah, and this baby is a VS one. Really expensive shit. Set me back *big* time, if you know what I mean."

My mom looked at him, stunned. She was a bit embarrassed by his disclosure of such personal details, not to mention that affordability had been an issue when it came to the selection. It was a nice ring, but hardly the bank-buster he was making it out to be. She had never even heard of VS1.

"Barbara initially picked out a chintzy ring," Ray continued, not batting an eyelash. "But I said no fiancée of mine is going around in anything less than VS one. That's the closest thing to flawless you can get without being Princess Diana, and my fiancée deserves only the best."

The sentiment warmed her enough to overlook the exaggeration. She knew he had been put down so many times by his mother that she wanted to let it slide. She told herself that he was just overcompensating, not trying to outright lie—sort of like Annie purposely fixing the bouquet toss so my mom would be the one to catch it. While not one hundred percent honest, nobody got hurt from bending the rules. Still, toward the end of the night, Mom still had Dad's "white lie" floating around in her head, even as he twirled her around the dance floor to the point of nausea.

"Ray, whoa! Slow down. You're making me sick."

"I love this song, Babe." He was ten speeds ahead of her, as though he were rushing on adrenaline. "I've been waiting all night for the band to play a good song. Wait till our wedding. Ours is going to be so much better than this one. Even our band will put this one to shame."

"That's terrible," Mom replied, and she meant it. Annie was her best friend and getting married wasn't a competition. He had already turned their honeymoon into one and made sure everyone thought her ring was as illustrious as Annie's, so Mom decided to not engage in his fantasy. Instead, as the band mercifully keyed down to a slow number, she put her arms around his neck and on tiptoe planted a kiss on his cheek. "You're sweet to want to give me only the best, Ray, but I don't need all that to be happy. All I need is you."

She wanted him to say "ditto" at least, but this one fell into the same category as wanting to hear him tell her she was beautiful—too petty to be a deal breaker.

"I want what they have, Barb," he said so softly he seemed to be talking more to himself than to her. "Only I want more, and I want you to have it, too." He was staring at Annie and Paul as they danced. She wasn't sure, but she thought his pupils grew so large they nearly swallowed his brown eyes until there was only a sea of black. Mom decided to ignore it—something she would come to regret. If she had taken heed of all the signs that were as clear as neon at night, surely she would have run as fast and as far as possible in the opposite direction. Instead she just tucked closer into his chest as he whispered fiercely, "And I'll get it. You better believe, I'll get it."

CHAPTER FIVE

Settling for Less

*"The minute you settle for less than you deserve,
you get even less than you settled for."*
—Maureen Dowd

A s with most weddings, there were a lot of last-minute details
to tend to before the big day—October 9, 1983. My Mom was
thankful that her mother took the lead. At the age of twenty-two,
she was quite content to let her handle most of the wedding plans.
They didn't have much time to plan the wedding in the first place,
since she and my dad had become engaged three months from the
day they got back together at Mrs. Campbell's funeral. Some of her
engaged friends took eighteen months or longer to get married,
and here they were—reunited, courted, engaged, and about to be
married—all within the same year. Their decision to move the
engagement process along obviously wasn't because she was pregnant, but neither of them saw the point in prolonging the engagement until the following year. Besides, as much as she loved my
grandparents, Aunt Robin, and Uncle Michael, Mom was ready to

get on with life as a married woman. One who had a place of her own, however modest, and could soon trade in her secretarial job to raise a big Catholic family, just as she'd dreamed of having once single life as a working girl in the city had lost its luster.

Of course they would marry at Our Lady of Grace and Dad's brother Danny would officiate the mass and ceremony.

Johnny Dee had begun to recede from the special spot she kept reserved for him in her heart. She was "all in" with Dad now, as she knew she should be. They secured the Crest Hollow Country Club on Long Island for their reception. It made my dad happy, especially since it was a much more exquisite place than where Annie and Paul had theirs.

Nanni, handled all the details such as flowers, centerpieces, and cake tasting, but there were a few traditions regarding the impending wedding day that she considered equally important. One was a bridal shower so Mom could receive all the necessary items that insure a long, happy marriage—Teflon frying pans, an arsenal of multifunctional pots, each one bigger than the other (including a twenty-quart sauce pot for sauce she had yet to learn how to make), and an electric knife. According to the giver of the gift, and affirmed by all the married attendees, the knife was considered a necessity for new husbands who had no experience with carving the Thanksgiving turkey.

The second tradition came as an embarrassing surprise at the shower when my mom opened a lavishly wrapped box from her mother. It was an exquisite peignoir. Mom said that she could feel the immediate blush that raced up her neck. Apparently this was an old custom that had been passed down to at least three generations of brides in Mom's family. Annie's mother had also followed this custom, so she had plenty of company, yet she felt painfully self-conscious. That was ridiculous, she knew, but brides were supposed to lose their virginity or consummate their brand-new marriage while draped in this fancy nightgown on their wedding night. And really, why would any mother want to pick out what her daughter was going to wear to have sex on her wedding night—and just what kind of daughter would feel comfortable wearing it?

At least that's what Mom wanted to blame for her discomfort, but she couldn't lie to herself. Her discomfort originated from another source—the basement and what had happened, and had *not* happened, in it.

"It's from France," Nanni told her, followed by a chorus of *ooh-la-las* from Mom's friends. "Well, actually, I found it at this amazing boutique on Nostrand Avenue that specializes in peignoirs and layettes, which will come in handy when the babies arrive!"

Mom said she managed a strained smile as she passed the box so the peignoir could be admired. She didn't want to think about the wedding night when she would reveal herself to my dad for the first time. Because he wanted to wait until they were married to have sex, the pressure would really be on, as opposed to something that just happened naturally. It made her nervous. The thing was, she hoped with all of her might that their wedding night would exceed her expectations. She was tired of worrying that she just wouldn't do it for him. Or what if he was terrible? She wasn't overly experienced, but Dad was still a virgin, and she could only hope that he would see enough videos at his stag party to know at least how things were supposed to work.

The "Peignoir Affair" as she came to think of it, bothered her enough after the wedding shower to broach the subject with my dad. It was about a week before the wedding, and she hoped that if she shared with him how jittery she was feeling about their wedding night he would, in turn, give her some insight on how he was feeling about it himself. Was he confident? Excited? Ready? Prepared? Curious? Not that she would actually expect a man, even though he was a virgin, to admit that the idea of sex with a woman made him anxious, but she was fishing for something, anything that would form a bond of intimacy between them in lieu of sex. If he did actually feel the same way about the mounting suspense, maybe she would even suggest they give it a try beforehand so they could both be relaxed and enjoy their wedding night. Besides, with the wedding only a week away, she figured they were as good as married.

Instead, my dad reasoned, "But with only a week to go, why would we make the time we've already waited be in vain? It's like running a marathon and then walking at mile twenty-five."

"You're right, Ray. I don't know what has gotten into me." His rationale was the complete opposite of what she had hoped for, and as much as she hated to admit it, she did see his point. She was also desperate to undo her suggestion for fear that he would decide she was a "bad girl" and call off the wedding at the last minute. Despite the apology/proposal, she couldn't quite forget his wounding words that night in this same space, my grandparents' basement.

You're not the marrying type.

As the echo of those words drowned out the conversation she and Dad were now having, she was thrown a life preserver in the form of a kiss. It was as if he were inside her head, sensing her insecurities and that she was going back to a place where she doubted his feelings for her and, more important, his opinions about her morals. He kissed her and the way he did it caught her off guard. This kiss was different. He kissed her sweetly, with feeling. He touched the tip of his nose to hers and said playfully, "Maybe that preview will be enough to hold you over."

But then something really amazing happened. He kissed her again. This time he took it to another level, something closer to genuine passion, and it was all she could do not to move him to the couch and miracle of miracles, she didn't have to. This time he was moving his hands to the small of her back and guiding her to the couch where he positioned her to straddle his lap as she faced him. Swept away by the unexpectedness of it all, she kissed him as hard as she had kissed her Johnny Dee. With her arms around the neck of this man who would be her husband, all she could think was, *I can't believe we're doing this. How did we get here?*

He didn't look at her, though. She knew this because she cheated and opened her eyes to gauge whether she had taken their spontaneous expression too far. No, she didn't think so.

"Is there anything you would like me to do?" It was hard to imagine they had been together for almost a year, and she had no idea if he enjoyed the sensation of getting a hickey. "Tell me what feels good to you," she asked again, sincere in her desire to know what she couldn't see in his eyes.

"Don't say anything and just keep kissing me."

Just for a moment she hesitated, then took the plunge. "Can I touch you?"

"No." In an instant, he left his intoxicated state like a patient who was just snapped out of a trance by his hypnotist. "Don't touch me. Just keep kissing."

She did as he asked and tried to kiss him passionately, but something had changed. She peeked at him again, and noticed that his eyes were squeezed together, as if he were in pain. His jaw was clenched and his hands had become tight fists, knotted into the skirt that had ridden above her hips.

"Ray, am I hurting you, or something?"

"No. Just keep kissing."

Her left leg had become a little numb, so she tried to reposition herself and noticed that his fly was undone. She took it as a cue to ignore his "don't touch" instruction. He slapped her hand away. "Just keep kissing. I will take care of myself."

Unsure of what he meant by that, she simply obeyed and kept kissing while he put his hand where hers had been heading, inside of his open pants. That's when she felt a rhythmic movement beneath her, but it didn't include her.

"I'm close," he panted, and in her peripheral vision she saw his right shoulder jerking in that same odd motion he made the night he was facing the corner in this very same basement—and just like that night, he didn't look at her once, even after he made a gasping sound and his movements stilled.

At that moment she was glad his eyes were shut because she was too confused and embarrassed to make eye contact as she quickly and quietly removed herself from his lap. She didn't want to say anything, because she didn't feel good about what had just happened. It was neither a consummation of their love nor a participation in a shared loving expression. She had wanted the experience to bring them closer together, but all it did was send her to a place far away, into the vault of memory where Johnny Dee's arms were wrapped around her as they lay together in the afterglow. *Johnny, where are you? Do you know I'm getting married?*

As Mom tried to make sense of the thoughts scrambling in her head, he suddenly opened his eyes, smiled broadly, and nonchalantly turned on the television before happily suggesting, "Let's order a pizza."

The irony wasn't lost on her that suddenly *she* felt like the inexperienced virgin even though she was the one who hadn't "saved" herself for marriage, who wasn't the "marrying type." But she had never seen anything like this, and he was acting so normal about it. What was she supposed to do with this information? At this point, Mom went into the (now normal to her) rationalizing. Was she making a mountain out of a molehill? Was this just something that she should expect if she was going to enter into a continuous sexual relationship? After all, she had only been with Johnny and they were kids when it happened. If she was going to keep her husband satisfied, maybe she needed to be more open minded about what married couples did in private. Maybe this was a normal thing married couples did all the time, and she just didn't know about it.

Although her instincts told her otherwise, she did not want to believe something weird and abnormal had just happened because if it had, she would be smart not to marry him, and the last thing she wanted to do was cancel the wedding—or confront him about what had happened and risk his calling it off himself. It was easier to believe that what had happened was an ingenious compromise on my dad's part. He had shown her the physical side of his nature while still managing to honor his religious convictions and save himself for marriage.

It was only a week until their wedding night, and she was more confused and nervous about it than ever. Mom told me that once again she should have been aware of a warning sign—she should have trusted her instincts. What 24-year-old man doesn't want to have sex with the love of his life?

It was two or three years after I first asked Mom to tell me about her past relationship with my dad that she was able to tell me about their wedding day and honeymoon. Some pain is so personal, is buried so deeply, it is difficult to acknowledge it. But sharing it—even with someone she loves, was nearly impossible.

After an eighteen-hour day of picture posing, limo rides, and meeting and greeting with more than 200 guests at the reception, Mom said that the sweetest moment of their wedding day came as they stood outside their apartment door. That's when Dad insisted on carrying her over the threshold. It amazed her that he still had enough energy and coordination to scoop her up and turn the door key in the lock at the same time.

With one arm wrapped around his neck, her free hand grasped the small canvas bag she had packed the night before. Her overnight bag was carefully planned—shampoo, conditioner, toothbrush, hairbrush, soap, makeup remover, and a change of clothes to wear on the flight to Hawaii the next day. Delicately folded on the top, so it wouldn't wrinkle, was the peignoir set.

Once inside the room, he kicked the back of the door shut with his heel and promptly deposited her on the floor.

When they finally entered their bedroom, he flopped diagonally across the bed, taking up so much space she would have to lie on top of him if she didn't want to sleep on the floor, the last thing she expected to hear was, "Jeez, I'm exhausted."

"Really?" Mom couldn't believe he would pull the equivalent of pleading a headache. "Well, um, I think I am going to wash up, and slip into something more . . . comfortable?"

"I shouldn't have had that last shot." He yawned loudly and said, "I feel like Rip Van Winkle. I can hardly keep my eyes open."

Mom said, "Why don't you get us a coke from the kitchen. I'll be ready when you get back."

With that, she ran to the bathroom and stared at her hair under the florescent track lighting of the cramped vanity. The giant bun that had taken a solid half hour to create was plastered to her head with about two cans of hairspray, and she desperately wanted to remove the cluster of bobby pins that had been stabbing her scalp since the hairdresser inserted them that morning. She didn't have time to mess with it. She needed to get out of her going-away dress and into the nightgown before he got back. After looking at herself in the mirror, she smiled. She had to admit she felt pretty confident. How could her new husband resist her in this tight-fitting, lacy outfit?

After she heard the turn of the doorknob signaling his return, followed by the slamming door, she knew that was her cue. This was it. She was legally Mrs. Ray Sheehan, about to have sex for the first time with her husband. As quickly as the memory of what happened in the basement emerged, she snuffed it. She wouldn't let herself think of anything but how sweet he smelled when they danced their first dance as husband and wife. She loved him for better or for worse, just as she had told him in front of 200 people. They had made it legal. Now they would make it official.

As she walked toward the bed, which Ray had already unmade, she wondered if he could get a clear picture of her in the darkened room. *Does he think I look pretty? Maybe even beautiful? Is he naked under the sheets?*

"Well, do you like it?" She said the words just as she had rehearsed them countless times in her head. Only then she sounded sex-kitten breathy instead of nervously high pitched and out of breath. Sitting gingerly on the edge of the bed, she wondered if he would prefer to sleep on the left side or the right after they made love.

"You know, Barb. That Coke didn't mix well with my stomach. And that last shot . . . I can't keep my eyes open."

"But it's our wedding night, and . . . well, I am wearing this for you."

"And it's beautiful. It really is."

"I'm glad you like it. And the woman in it, too?" She wasn't above fishing at this point.

"Of course," he assured her with a little squeeze to her hand. "But we have an eleven-hour flight at eight in the morning. It's close to two a.m. We'll have plenty of time when we get to Hawaii." And with that, he kissed her on the cheek, let go of her hand, and rolled to the far side of the bed.

Mom stared at his back until he began to snore loudly. She wondered if it was a fake snore to make her think he was sleeping. It didn't matter. Either way, the outcome was the same. She retreated to the bathroom, where she tackled her agony one bobby pin at a time.

CHAPTER SIX

Reality

*"Learn to see things as they really are,
not as we imagine they are."*
—Vernon Howard

My parents spent their one-day anniversary on a Pan Am flight to Maui where they would spend nine nights and ten days. It should have been idyllic. By the time their plane landed in Hawaii, Mom was prepared for the excuses. She figured that my dad would have a jet lag problem, or he might be still hung over from that shot. She felt like a sham when they were greeted by the staff at the lavish hotel with the enthusiastic congratulations and sly winks reserved for newlyweds.

She knew what they were thinking; the same thing that everyone at home presumed was going on. She wished she could be excited, but the wedding night rejection still stung. The room was beautiful, but she would have taken their little bedroom of the night before with sincere declarations of love and earnest passion, over a heart-shaped sunken tub that she would probably end up soaking in all by herself. The peignoir certainly hadn't done the trick and she was tired of trying.

My dad surprised her by asking her, in a seductive voice, to get into something more comfortable. She didn't have to be asked twice.

When she emerged from the bathroom wearing the peignoir, the blackout shades had been drawn against the setting sun and the air conditioner had been cranked up. Dad was sitting on the edge of the bed with his knees clenched together and his hands clasped in his lap. She realized that he was even more nervous than she was.

He asked her to hit the lights, and even though that wouldn't have been her preference, she also knew that the moment was precarious and she wasn't going to make an issue of it.

As with many monumental events, the buildup, the anticipation of it, was the best part. The actual event was awkward, and when her peignoir had finally served its purpose, she told herself that practice, after all, makes perfect and they just needed more of it.

However, their honeymoon wound up being a series of distractions from sex and intimacy, as my parents took turns inflicting drama on each other. First, they contended with jet lag issues. Dad was more of a trouper than she was, but they both took about two days before feeling acclimated and normal enough to give sex another go. After another lackluster experience, she woke the following morning to find Dad missing from bed. Mom called his name, then checked the bathroom and found no trace of him. She frantically pulled back the shades and spotted him walking the beachfront property of the hotel. It was quite a distance away, but still, she recognized his gait. His walking turned to pacing. He didn't look like a man who had awakened early to relish a sunrise; he was frantic.

Mom raced out of the room to find out what was wrong and once she was close enough to be heard over the rush of waves, she shouted, "Are you okay?" When he didn't answer, she ran down to the beach. When she reached him, she could see something in his eyes she'd never seen before—defeat.

"I can't find it. My ring. It's gone."

"Your wedding ring?" She'd never seen Dad this vulnerable, and it was impossible not to feel compassion for him when he nodded with a look of misery.

"I realized yesterday it was gone and hoped you wouldn't notice. I was up half the night, retracing my steps from yesterday and figured it had to be lost on the beach since we spent the whole day here." As an aspiring detective, he thought he should have been able to solve this mystery and was clearly frustrated by his failure.

Mom couldn't help wondering if this was a sign that they shouldn't be married. This incident haunted her for their entire marriage—the thought that she should have left when God and the ocean took away the wedding ring. My father lost other wedding rings over the years, and Mom always bought him a new one.

After they called off the search, Dad became sullen, and Mom was homesick. Neither of them were having fun. The incident put a damper on their collective moods, and they couldn't pull each other out of the rut. By day four, Mom missed Nanni and Aunt Robin so much she wanted to call home just to hear their voices.

"Cut the cord already," my dad snapped at her. "And stop

being so unworldly. I plan on traveling a lot, Barbara, so you better get used to being away from them."

Mom sucked it up and determined to finish off the week without acting like a "baby." She spent the rest of the honeymoon wondering if it was her fault that he wasn't in the mood. She counted down the days until my grandparents would meet them at the arrivals gate at JFK. She hoped that she and Dad would find their groove once they were settled into their new apartment.

Halloween was upon them when they got back to New York, and some of the stores in the mall had already started decorating for Christmas. The just-married Sheehans settled into their one-bedroom apartment, which was so small they had to kneel on the bed in order to pull out the dresser drawers. Mom started thinking about Christmas—their first Christmas together. A much-needed and welcome thought since what could be better than being a newlywed during the holidays? She thought about a Thanksgiving turkey (complete with an electric knife), Christmas tree ornaments engraved with "Our First Christmas 1983," and a room full of relatives toasting the newlyweds with raised champagne flutes.

When my parents initially discussed where they would live after getting married, they agreed the logical place would be Howard Beach. Mom couldn't see them living in Brooklyn, where Dad's family lived, and they both knew that once the babies came, it would make sense to be close to her family. Mom's commute into the city wouldn't change and Howard Beach wasn't far from Dad's precinct, which would most likely change once he made detective anyway. However, after his reaction to her honeymoon homesickness and her "dependency" on her family, Mom was afraid he might change his mind about living in an apartment close to my grandparents' house. Maybe he'd decide that moving to Brooklyn would be a way to get her out of her comfort zone—to prep her for a more "worldly" life, which he looked forward to having. Her relief was immense when, instead, he said that moving her away from her family would just condemn him to a life filled with her whining and nagging. She knew he was probably right.

Mom wanted desperately to host at least one of the holidays that year, but there would be no way to fit both sides of the family in the apartment. Besides, more than likely, Dad would have to spend much of the holiday season at work, taking extra overtime whenever he could get it. There would be plenty of other years to celebrate and host, and they both looked forward to inheriting at least some of the holiday duties, once they bought a bigger place and really settled down. Between her salary at the bank and his base, plus overtime, and the prospect of a promotion, she hoped they would be able to make that happen soon.

Mom could live with the reality of Dad's inflexible and erratic schedule and the fact that their first Christmas would most likely not be spent together, but the one thing she couldn't do without was a Christmas tree in the living room. The place was crowded with just a couch and coffee table, so adding a Douglas fir to the mix seemed impossible, but mom was determined. They got a real tree, which took up most of their living space and shed needles all over the floor, but it made Mom happy and that seemed to make Dad happy in return.

"Where will we put the presents? There isn't any room." Dad

laughed at the sight of his new wife trying to reach around the tree only to realize the front was all she could possibly decorate. "Well, since we can't fit any *real* gifts under the tree, maybe I will just have to put a bow around me and plant myself under the tree."

"That's not a bad idea," Dad said, as he gently touched the soft waves of her hair. His touch was unexpected and rare, and it gave her hope that they were finally off to a better start. They had only been intimate one time since returning from the honeymoon, which made three times total. The lack of their intimate connection worried her. Dad wasn't even affectionate when they said goodnight—no kisses or hugs or words of love. It just didn't seem normal to her—not that their whirlwind courtship had been all that normal either, now that she had the perspective of a little distance. She had the uncomfortable feeling that they should have gotten to know each other better before rushing into marriage. This kind of thinking made her uncomfortable, so rather than ask Dad why he would rather fall asleep in front of the television than in bed with her in his arms, she let it go yet again. What was done was done. They were married now, so she would focus on Christmas and on making him happy.

After only two-and-a-half months of marriage, Mom realized that being a cop's wife wasn't as glamorous as she had expected. All of the Sheehans and the Henrys were proud of having a police officer and soon-to-be detective in the family. Of course it was a badge of honor for Mom too, but there were sacrifices Dad made that she would now have to make also. The severity of her responsibilities as a cop's wife didn't hit her until Christmas Day, when she spent the whole of it alone with her family and felt so . . . unmarried. There weren't any champagne toasts to the happy couple or waking up together on Christmas morning to open presents. She just hadn't prepared herself for how much solo time she would have to endure, and while Dad promised it would all pay off, he did warn her that once he became a detective his hours would become even more unpredictable, as he would have to be on call if there were a homicide.

To cope with adjusting to their unique relationship, Mom adopted the policy of quality over quantity. If she couldn't spend a lot of time with Dad, she would make sure the time they did spend together was special. That first Christmas night, Dad was due home in a few hours, and she thought it would be amazing to create a special Christmas memory for them to share—starting with a red satin baby doll nightie one of her girlfriends had given her at the wedding shower. It didn't have the negative associations she had attached to the peignoir, and so a few minutes before he said he would be home, she slipped on the nightie and positioned herself on the living room floor beneath the Christmas tree. The lack of space forced her into a sideways leaning position, and she practiced holding her weight up on her elbow and forearm. She tried dangling an ornament in her free hand and debated about how to greet him.

She kept her eyes on the door for some time, but after a while began to feel foolish. Besides that, she was uncomfortable. Her arm had fallen asleep. She got up and tried to shake the feeling back into it. Then, thinking surely he would be home any minute, she tried a different position under the tree.

When an hour had passed and she couldn't stand the silence or discomfort any longer, she got up and turned the television on to watch the news. She couldn't imagine what was keeping him. After the news, Carson came on, and she decided to make a left-over turkey sandwich. She then started to worry in earnest, afraid that something had happened to him and that he might not come home at all.

She hadn't thought about that before—that there was a very good possibility every time Dad went to work, he might not come back. He was a patrolman in Brooklyn at a busy precinct, and it had never occurred to her that the possibility of becoming a widow could be added to the long list of negative things that went with being married to a cop.

A chill ran through her at the thought of why Dad wasn't home yet. She changed into her flannel pajamas and curled up in a ball in the bed. She fell asleep praying that Dad would be delivered safely back to her.

Sometime in the wee hours, she got out of the bed to go to the bathroom and realized he must be home. She hadn't heard him come in, but the big gun he wore on his hip was on the bathroom sink. Having the gun left out in plain sight like that made her very uncomfortable. She couldn't understand the way he treated it as cavalierly as tossing a set of car keys around. She really didn't like guns or know much about them beyond the fact that they were dangerous, but Dad called her silly whenever she expressed her concerns. He also found it humorous that she referred to one gun as the "big gun" because she couldn't remember the technical name for the piece, and that differentiated it from the "little gun" he usually wore on his ankle.

She saw the light from the other side of the wall where the living room was. She didn't know if she was relieved that he was safe or angry with him for worrying her. She opted to go with whatever she felt when she saw him. This is the way it went:

"Where were you?" It was an accusation, a demand to know, and came out sharper than she intended.

"Merry Christmas to you, too." He got up from the couch and walked over to her.

"You couldn't call? I thought you were dead."

"I got a drug collar tonight. Made a big arrest."

Mom recognized this as her cue to congratulate him and listen to his instant replay of the night's events, but she didn't want to hear about it. She wanted him to apologize, and then promise it would never happen again.

He was irritated with her lack of response and said, "Do you know how many hours of paperwork I had to do? I got some overtime out of it, at least."

"You couldn't pick up the phone at your desk and let me know?"

"I didn't want to wake you."

"I wasn't asleep."

"Well, how the hell was I supposed to know that?"

"Why are you getting mad at *me*? You're the one who should've called, Ray. You aren't a single guy anymore. You have a wife who worries about you." She didn't want to tell him about the red nightie and the romantic plans as a last-ditch effort to have some sort of Christmas together. There was already a wedge between them and pushing the issue wasn't going to solve anything. Neither was his continued silence.

If communication was key to a successful marriage, as Nanni had told her, as well as several of the women at her shower, Mom had a bad feeling that they were already in trouble. Flustered and grasping at anything to keep the conversation going, she blurted, "The least you could do is stop leaving your gun in the bathroom—and on the dresser, too. You know that bothers me."

"Barbara, what do you expect? I'm a cop. Do you know how irrational you sound?"

He was turning this on her, twisting everything around. But before she could remind him that this was all his fault, he was making her feel like the guilty one. "Now, let me get this straight. You don't want me to come home late *or* make arrests *or* put in overtime? And now, no guns in the house? What am I supposed to do, retire? Give up my career and go flip burgers at McDonalds?"

"That's not what I said."

"Yes, it is."

He was putting words in her mouth, but she couldn't manage the mental gymnastics to refute him. Mom had seen a show recently on TV, maybe it was *20/20* or *Nightline,* she couldn't recall, but it was some talk show and the guest was a psychologist who talked about the term "passive-aggressive." What the psychologist had to say really bothered her because a lot of the traits he described—such as envying those who were more fortunate, exaggerating, being negative in a covert way and a lot of other things she didn't want to hear—came awfully close to some of Dad's behavior. The psychologist also said it had a lot to do with how kids were raised; if they'd had to repress their feelings growing up or sugarcoat being angry in a bad environment. Mom wondered if it was the same for adults, because that's the way she felt at that moment. She hoped not—and she sure didn't want Dad to be one because it sounded like they could be messed up people who had a way of messing with the other people around them. She wished she hadn't seen that show. She thought that the guy would probably say anything to get on TV, and you couldn't believe everything you heard or saw on television. She thought she should just stick with the sit-coms to get a laugh and keep her spirits up instead of listening to "experts" who put disturbing thoughts in her head. She would take the advice an elderly aunt had given her. *Sometimes keeping the peace is more important than being right.*

"Okay, Ray. Fine, you're right. Let's just get some sleep." Then there was that other piece of advice she'd heard from every happily married couple she knew, "Never go to bed angry."

It only took a few months to fall into a married lull. Mom craved routine, and she got it. Now that she was married she didn't go out with the single girls after work. All she did was get up, go to work, and come home to spend night after night alone. No more dates, no more hanging out with the wives and girlfriends of Dad's cop buddies, and worst of all, no more Annie, who never returned her calls. It was strange because they'd been so close and ever since she'd gotten back from Hawaii, not one single message she'd left on Annie's answering machine had been returned. She'd go shopping alone on the weekends, come back to find Dad watching TV, and anxiously ask him, "Did Annie call?" and he'd say, "Nah, she must be too busy being married and taking care of her husband— like you should be taking care of me. What's for dinner?"

She would then go make dinner and hope he wouldn't say it stunk or she needed to take cooking lessons from his mother—that he'd instead relay the message that she had done okay by either saying nothing or not making a face as if he'd put something foul in his mouth. She, in turn, would squelch the impulse to call Annie one more time.

Dad eventually told her that she was making a nuisance out of herself—that Paul had said as much when they ran into each other at the home improvement store. Although, whatever he would be doing there if not on duty was a mystery to her; it wasn't like they had home projects lined up in the tiny apartment that felt smaller by the day.

Mom told herself that maybe he was just a little jealous of the relationship she had with Annie, so either he had exaggerated what Paul said, or maybe he simply made it up. He did that sometimes, but she had become careful not to call him on his "little white lies" because he always twisted things around. She would become defensive, and then she'd feel like the bad guy and ultimately apologize for not believing him. If there was a chance that Paul really did say she was being a nuisance, then it could be that Paul was the one who had some jealousy issues and the last thing she wanted to do was put a strain on their marriage. She couldn't believe that Annie and Paul might be having marital problems, but then again, everyone at work and in the family thought she and Dad were happy as could be. That wasn't by accident. She was very good at acting as though everything was just great in her life. Mom found that acting took a lot of mental and emotional energy. She longed for someone she could confide in, and without Annie, there just wasn't anyone. The closest person she had was her sister, Robin, but she just couldn't bring herself to tell her how lonely she was; how it seemed that Dad was always working and his schedule conflicted with her work schedule, which made them more like two ships passing in the night than a newlywed couple. Of course, there was the issue of their sex life, or lack thereof, which she was too ashamed about to share with anyone.

About six months into their marriage, it took all of her acting skill not to let Robin see her pain when she mentioned that she'd recently run into Johnny Dee.

"I saw him at the butcher. Can you believe he remembered me?"

Dying to know more, Mom managed nonchalantly to follow up with, "That's cool. Did he ask about me?"

"He said he heard you were married."

She couldn't believe that Johnny knew. But then it wasn't unusual for such things to spread around Howard Beach like wildfire. Of course there had been the wedding announcement in the paper, so perhaps it was more a matter of how could he *not* know? She hadn't heard anything or read anything about him moving on, but that didn't mean anything. A selfish part of her hoped that he hadn't.

"Is he with anyone?" Mom wanted so badly for the answer to be no.

"I didn't think to ask. But you know what he *did* tell me?" If she noticed that her big sister was hanging on her every word, Robin didn't show it. "He said, 'Tell Barbara I am happy for her even though my heart is breaking.' "

Mom's thought was, *Oh, God, what have I done?*

Johnny's words stuck with Mom like a song—and a curse. Knowing that Johnny still loved her made her feel more alive than she had felt since high school. But when she returned home to an empty house night after night, she died all over again. She turned to food for comfort, and the results were not flattering. Once she could no longer fit in her favorite skirt, and my father pointed out that she was getting fat, she knew she had to snap herself out of it. If she couldn't have Johnny, and she couldn't have a normal sex life with a husband who said mean things to her, she decided to do something daring to put some zest back into her dull existence.

"I'm getting a tattoo." Mom announced her idea to my father while he was preoccupied with the Mets on one of his few Saturdays off. That's when he liked to indulge his favorite pastime of yelling at whatever sports team was playing—and better them than at her, was Mom's reasoning. He had begun raising his voice when she made a simple mistake, like not buying the right flavor of ice cream, or worse, forgetting to buy any at all. Wrong flavor, raised voice. No ice cream at all, watch out! So she had learned to pay close attention and not be the "fucking idiot" he said she was if she forgot.

"I'm getting a tattoo," she repeated, this time a little louder, wondering if he even noticed she was in the room. Surely a tattoo would get his attention.

"Over my dead body." He didn't take his eyes off the game. With his arms crossed and his legs up on the coffee table, he was stoic, calm, and confident she would back down.

"I thought just a little rose on my ankle would be cute." While she didn't like his tone, in a warped way she was happy to have elicited a response from him. Negative attention was better than no attention at all. She felt like a kid who acts out to stop being ignored, and would take what she could get.

"Tattoos are for sluts! It's bad enough I had to make an honest woman out of you, but no wife of mine tramps around with any marks on her body, do you hear me?"

"You're not my father!"

"But I *am* your husband."

"Well, you don't act like one."

"What is that supposed to mean?"

Mom saw this as her opening, and she was ready. "What it means is that I have been sitting alone in this tiny, claustrophobic apartment, eating dinner by myself. I don't see any friends, work is driving me crazy, and you aren't around for family functions or even to go see a movie. You work all of the time, and you don't bring home any money for overtime. When you're not working, you go out with who knows who and where or you're tired and mean and say stuff that hurts my feelings! How much am I sup-posed to put up with? If this is how our marriage is going to go for the rest of our lives, tell me now, Ray, because it's not for me. We both deserve better. Are you unhappy? Do you want out? I just want to stop living like this. It's not what I signed up for."

He finally looked away from the game and straight at her. His emotionless eyes locked with hers, and he pointed his finger at her. "Oh yes, you did. The day you said 'I do' in front of God, my brother the priest, and every other witness there, you signed up for life. It's an unbreakable contract in the eyes of the church, and I will not be excommunicated because you got some crazy hair up your ass. So I suggest you shut your stupid trap, go make dinner, and don't make the mistake of bringing this up again. If you understand me, and if you have a brain, you will nod your head."

Her heart was pounding like mad. Despite the screams of "No!" inside her head, she managed to nod. "Good," he said. And with that, he turned his attention back to the game. "Go make me some chicken wings, would you? It's been a long week, and I'm beat."

CHAPTER SEVEN

The Monster Within

*"No passion so effectually robs the mind
of all its powers of acting and reasoning as fear."*
—EDMUND BURKE

When Mom first dreamed of married life, she thought of a house with a picket fence, four children, dinner parties, holidays around their dining room table, Brownies and Boy Scouts, and a variety of intramural sports for the kids. However, by the time they marked their one-year anniversary, all she could think about was pain relief from her constant headaches. It didn't take much to figure out there was a correlation between how hard she tried to make their marriage work and her migraines.

She wished she could get inside of my father's head, and yet she had a sense of trepidation regarding what she might find if she actually managed to get in there. Did she really want to know why he had married her if he found touching her so distasteful? There were those rare instances, such as when he had gently touched her hair by the Christmas tree, that she clung to as evidence that he must bear some true affection for her. The contradictory aspects of his nature that she thought she would eventually understand had seemed to intensify. She wondered if she was too dumb to discern the reasons for the things he did and said—like when he called her stupid and self-absorbed while pointing his finger at her as if it were a gun.

One time he forgot to put his gun down before he started to do his finger waving, which totally freaked Mom out. For a moment she believed he was really going to shoot her. But when she started screaming, "Don't shoot me!" he immediately put down the gun and rushed over to her.

"Oh, Babe, I'm sorry. I didn't mean to scare you like that," he assured her. He even hugged her, and she latched onto him like a leech because she was so starved for an expression of love and some sign she wasn't totally repugnant.

The weight she had been gaining lowered her self-esteem, and she craved reassurance that she was still pretty and not the disgusting pig he thought she was. Not that he had called her that exactly, but she felt that's what he thought whenever they ate together. But after he scared her with the gun, he became a little less insulting, and for a while, he kept the gun out of sight. Mom said it was almost as if he had scared himself, such as someone who goes on a bender, and then stops drinking for a while to make sure he isn't developing a problem. That was at least something—he didn't have a drinking problem. Mom said she had not seen him inebriated at that point except one time, and he had done something so weird she decided it had just been her imagination. He fell asleep sucking his thumb.

There was one thing that gave my parents the semblance of a genuine marriage—they both wanted a house. The more closed in Mom felt, the more chaotic her world seemed to become, and it probably was another contributing factor to the headaches. As for my dad, it meant a lot to him that they wouldn't be "left behind" when so many other young couples in the community were moving on to houses and kids. Mom realized it really was important to him when he promised they wouldn't sign another lease on the apartment. He was moving up quickly at the police department, and with each paycheck, they got closer to buying their own home. They moved from the small apartment to a condominium, but that didn't satisfy my dad's need for more. Not long after they moved into the condo, my dad was wanting out.

When they first saw the house in Howard Beach, they immediately knew it was meant to be theirs. Mom loved the block with its peaceful tree line. The three-bedroom, one-and-a-half bath was near shopping, transportation, and just a few blocks away from my grandparents' house, and in the vicinity of Our Lady of Grace Church. Mom could already imagine the church bells ringing as she prepared brown-bag lunches for the troop of kids she'd be sending off to Our Lady of Grace's grammar school.

Outside, the house was narrow with a pointed roof, but inside, it had so much potential. Although not too handy, my father began to count the ways he could upgrade the kitchen, break down walls for a roomier basement, and build a deck out to the backyard. He saw the house as a great investment in real estate, while Mom viewed it as an investment in *them*.

She and my dad began to communicate through the house, as if the little property were a mediator. Something had changed and it was good—they had common ground and common interests, and for a while the house, and their combined responsibility to it, became their baby. Mom's headaches slacked off in direct proportion to the time she and Dad invested themselves into their nest. Their marriage felt stable in a way it hadn't before; the foundation of their home provided something concrete on which to build the harmonious partnership she had longed for.

Dad was so proud to show off their place, and it upset Mom when his mother made a disparaging remark about it needing work. Naturally, owning a home would mean the world to my dad after he had grown up living in his relatives' rentals, and my Grandma Edith's unkindness reminded Mom of why she needed to be patient with Dad when he said or did hurtful things. Mom had received her fair share of nurturing and encouragement, which was something he had never been given. She could only presume that it had been that way for his brothers Danny and Vincent as well. It continued to amaze her how well adjusted those two appeared to be, given her knowledge of their upbringing. She was sorry that she couldn't honestly say the same for my dad. Living with someone, she had learned, was a far cry from dating him. There were habits and ticks and odd little mannerisms people have that they probably don't even realize they possess—like thumb sucking. Mom thought it had to have been her imagination. And spending inordinate amounts of time in the bathroom. Mom would tell him he had been in there over an hour and she had to get ready for work. He would respond with, "I've been in here ten minutes max. Stop imagining things and get your watch fixed."

Sometimes she wondered if there was something broken inside of my father. But the way he behaved after they bought the house made her think she had indeed let her imagination go haywire. Even if he wasn't affectionate, he had begun to surprise her with little trinkets, and she was grateful that he was once again willing to share some of his social circle from work—just as he had when they were engaged and he played softball. Mom desperately wanted his co-workers' wives to accept her, since she had lost touch with most of her own friends. Losing Annie's friendship was terrible, but she just didn't know how to go about getting her back without making Dad angry. Better not to rock the boat, she had learned, and with things going so well, that was the last thing she wanted to do.

Although Dad had gone from the philosophy of saving one's self for marriage to sex being reserved for procreation, he did want to do his Catholic duty and produce some more little Catholics. Not that he needed a reason or an excuse to travel, but he suggested they have one last hoorah before they started their family, and they joined two other couples for a getaway in St. Martin.

The beautiful high cliffs and low lands of St. Martin struck Mom as apt symbols of her marriage. There were the dizzying highs of a wedding and buying a first house, to all the low points that lay in between. But here in St. Martin, things were up again, with Dad taking her dining and dancing; rotating with the other couples to host happy hours in each other's rooms; renting a car and driving to the French side and lounging at outdoor tropical watering holes off the beaten path; and ordering beer from women who spoke with exotic accents. My dad's bright mood escalated with each new excursion they took and there, on an island paradise surrounded by their new friends, he made my mom laugh again.

At Mom's bridal shower, an elderly woman had taken her aside to say that marriage could be like a yo-yo, because you were likely to fall in and out of love with your spouse as life changed and the two of you changed with it. Yes, there would be tough times, but the reward for sticking them out was falling in love many times with the same, but different, man. It was on that trip to St. Martin when Mom accepted that she had fallen out of love with her husband—if she had ever truly been in love with him to begin with. Barely in her twenties at the time, what did she know? But that was no excuse to bail out when the going got tough.

The comparison of marriage to a yo-yo hit home while Dad was on a Jet Ski. He thrived on the rush of new experiences and while his impulsiveness could be a liability in terms of Mom's comfort zone at home, on trips it was the wind in their sails. He inspired her and the two other couples to join him in renting Jet Skis, even though he had never been on one in his life.

As he hoisted his leg over the Jet Ski, he lost his balance and slowly tipped over to the left side, despite the rest of the group successfully managing their balance on the first try.

"I think I just pissed my bathing suit," he admitted loudly, as he tried to gain control over his flailing arms after his third spill into the choppy water. "I'm such a clumsy fucker compared to you guys! Who knew this shit was so hard!"

Mom said that his language was typically colorful, and at this point in their marriage he even applied it himself, which helped her not to take it as personally when he used the same language on her. But on this trip he hadn't once called her dumb or stupid or a bitch—in fact, he'd hardly called her any bad names at all since they had moved into their beloved new house.

With each dunk he took, her heart remembered the man that perhaps she had been in love with when they said their vows. Even if not, she could easily be in love with this wild and crazy guy who made everyone laugh until their sides ached.

As my dad packed up his suitcase, Mom couldn't explain the ominous sense of doom she felt. She was sad as she thought of how she would miss all of it; St Martin, the great time they had together, and the different guy she was married to while they were there.

And that she did. Reality touched down simultaneously with the wheels of their plane on the runway at JFK. By the time they reached home, some sort of vacation amnesia had set in; their island fantasy was reduced to a mirage. They unpacked and ate dinner in silence. Mom thought about what type of window treatments to buy for the living room.

I was born first, and really have no memories until Raymond was born, three and one-half years later. I have seen pictures, of course, and things looked "normal," but then they always did in pictures. Mom said she considered it a miracle they conceived either of us. Their sex life was methodical and intentional with one goal in mind: to get pregnant. It was also highly sporadic and after Raymond was born, essentially nonexistent. With Dad's new detective status, sometimes Mom would go a few days without seeing him, and then he would slip into bed at two or three o'clock in the morning, supposedly after a homicide investigation—although she was beginning to doubt that, because he wasn't receiving overtime compensation for the long hours he was away from home. Still, she wished for him at least to put an arm around her—but he didn't. She began to feel like one of those experimental baby monkeys kept in a cage to see how they would react after being isolated for a long time, and the results were not good. Monkeys, like humans, need a certain amount of nurturing; without it, they become antisocial, and are barely able to function when put in a normal environment.

Mom felt that she really needed to quit watching so much TV. Especially those talk shows like the new one with Oprah Winfrey. She liked Oprah as a personality, but the issues her shows often covered, things like domestic abuse, made her uncomfortable. She wasn't sure why domestic abuse would make her uncomfortable, because Dad had never hit her, *yet*. Once the newness of the house had worn off and I was born, he had reverted to some of his old ways by yelling at her for little things that ticked him off and calling her bad names again like bitch, asshole and stupid. Although, as much as she hated to admit it, she had let herself go. She was so close to being fat from the additional weight she had gained from her pregnancies that her girlfriends from high school wouldn't recognize her.

She didn't have any girlfriends at all now. For some reason she hadn't clicked with the other cops' wives enough to hang out with them, and at this point she doubted Annie would even want to be around her, since according to my father she'd become a "depressed sack of shit." Mom felt that she was such a mess she could hardly bear her own company, so why would anyone else want to be around her?

Raymond and I were Mom's life, and she knew that we loved her unconditionally. We needed her as much as she needed us. She would make a field trip out of going to the supermarket. To make the excursion last as long as possible, she would take little steps down the canned food isle. She would pick up different products and read the labels from front to back, since she had nowhere else better to be. She had traded in her fulltime day job for homemaking and part-time work, which is what she thought she wanted, but after a while, she wondered if she was good for anything at all.

From watching *Oprah,* she knew she probably needed some type of professional counseling, but that's not the sort of thing her family did, or my father would ever approve of. For once she was sorry not to be more anonymous in their parish, because she didn't feel like she could unload her private burden in confession. My dad's brother could be on the other side of the confessional booth, and she was sure he didn't want to hear about the problems she had with my dad or his mother; or that she felt worthless and depressed, but why she wasn't sure because she didn't know how to articulate the confusion she felt.

Instead, help came from her sister-in-law, Linda, who is married to Dad's twin brother, Vincent. She had noticed the shift in Mom's usual upbeat personality. She and Mom saw a lot of each other, and my cousin Kathleen is only a year younger than I am. Linda and Vincent were nice to us, and pleasant to be around.

Because she was married to a man who shared so much DNA with Dad, Mom hoped that Linda could understand on a visceral level what she was experiencing. But Vincent wasn't like Dad. He supported his wife emotionally—he held her hand and talked highly of her. Mom envied her. She admitted this to Linda one time during a family trip to Disney World, when Linda had confronted her about being so quiet. It was hard for Linda to believe that Mom felt so lonely and emotionally abandoned by Dad, even when Mom explained that their marriage had started out with an aura of separateness. But Linda was sympathetic and validated her feelings by not judging them. She assured Mom that with all she had to take care of, it was perfectly normal for her to experience some burnout, especially since Dad wasn't picking up any of the slack.

Burned out was exactly how Mom felt. She was tired of always looking harried and never partaking in adult conversation anymore. She wanted a husband, a lover, a friend, and instead of whining about the fact that she didn't have any of those things in Dad, she felt that she needed to gain some control over the situation. The problem was that she didn't know how. She was caught up in a hopeless cycle that had resulted in a sea of self-pity. Yes, she was burned out, but she was also sick and tired of feeling sorry for herself. She felt that she had to take some responsibility for it; she didn't think it was something she could pin entirely on my dad.

Mom told Linda she knew that she had to get her act together, and Linda agreed—she told her that life is what you make it. She then pointed at my dad, who was trying to get Raymond's carriage on the Monorail, and told her that her life was right there. They gave my dad a hand with the carriage and boarded the Monorail, only my dad lost a flip-flop in the process. He clowned around about losing it and having to borrow one of Raymond's, and endeared himself to my mom once again. He had the uncanny ability to tug at her heartstrings at the very moment she considered them cut. It was as though he had a sixth sense that only worked on vacation—some sort of knowing when she was on the verge of giving up on them, and if he could make her laugh then he could make her stay. It was a different tactic and it worked on a different emotional level than frightening her into acquiescence, as he had that day over the tattoo. Different tactic but same motive, she told herself, because he didn't want to lose her. She also told herself that the real Ray was the one who showed up on vacation, not the one who could behave badly after a long day at work; and she had to cut him some slack because he hadn't been taught better at home.

But Vincent had? She thought that somehow she had to stop comparing the two brothers. She had to appreciate life as it was instead of complaining about what it wasn't. She would quit focusing on the things she wanted, so she could better want what she already had.

Mom traded her depression for quiet resignation. By the time I was four and Raymond was nine months old, she had been able to introduce a rhythm into our lives that made it possible to juggle one pre-school-aged child, an infant, a part-time job and a house, all without feeling like a desperate loser. She had also assumed the responsibility of my dad's demand that his home be "kept like a palace."

Although she had dealt with the depression, the escalating anxiety regarding the state of our house was another matter. She became obsessed with making sure the furniture was dustless, the rugs vacuumed, the kitchen sink sanitized, and all our toys put away before Dad got home. But she never really knew when that would be, so she remained in a constant state of preparedness, like a soldier anticipating an impromptu inspection of her bunk.

Once Dad made sergeant, his stress level went through the roof, and Mom's anxiety rose several notches as well. Apparently my dad started bringing work home with him, but it wasn't the usual kind of work other people bring home from the office.

The first day he came home in the middle of the day, on the pretext of having lunch, he had a videotape that he popped into the VCR and told Mom to "check it out." She was horrified—it was a video of a gruesome crime scene he was working. She begged him to turn it off. He told her to shut the fuck up and watch it so she could better appreciate what he did.

Mom gagged as she watched it, and he told her that she would get used to it; that it was just another day at the office for him. Then he told her to make him a sandwich while he took some notes, and then she could keep him company while he ate.

Mom felt threatened and terribly frightened of what he would be capable of after watching those videos. He could commit the perfect crime he was always talking about and threatening Mom with, and now he was even taking notes. But she did as she was told, and averted her eyes while he pointed out the various aspects of his job in examining the dead bodies, bloodstained rooms, and unidentifiable body parts on the tape that he had helped record at the scene of the crime.

So committed was he to his work that the tapes trumped yelling at the Mets as his favorite pastime. He particularly enjoyed the added benefit of being able to press PAUSE and REWIND on the videos—especially when they were extra gory. Mom pleaded with him not to do that, but he just told her that she should be more supportive and grateful that he took his work so seriously. Raymond and I never saw any of the videos because Mom always made us leave the room—for which I am thankful.

This new obsession of my father's became the norm at our house. Mom said that when she realized she could go to mass, then come home and block out what was playing on the VCR if she ran the vacuum, she was more disturbed by her ability to shut it out than his insistence on bringing it in. This was part of his job and to do it effectively a cop would have to build up some resistance. But that wouldn't be normal in a housewife like my mom. She said that it was warping her sense of what was normal and what was not.

She felt certain that what he was doing went against police policy—like taunting other drivers on the road during off hours, which he had begun to do again. If it was against police policy, she had to keep this secret because if she told anyone they might tell someone else, or even decide to report my father themselves. She could not let that happen. She couldn't even think of how devastating and destructive that would be—and she wasn't just thinking in terms of finances. My father defined himself by his public position of authority, and the fallout at home, especially if he fingered my mom as the originating source for his being disciplined or fired, would be beyond devastating. He hadn't hit her—yet—but he had begun to clench and unclench his fists when she was around, and she had a bad feeling that if something pushed him over the edge, she would be the one to suffer the weight of his wrath.

She didn't tell anyone about the tapes. Neither did she say any-thing about the photos he started bringing home—graphic still shots of the dead bodies he was investigating for the crime scene division. But he began to show them off to my mom's family—a thinly disguised threat to my mom that this could happen to her. Mom's horror was met with his fury. Did she *not* understand the pride he took in being in charge of the mutilated remains?

She did not understand, and with each crime committed, he brought photos from the case file home as if they were blue rib-bons. He seemed to take a perverse pleasure in waving the "trophy photos" in her face while scoffing down a cold-cut hero and bottle of beer.

My father's frustration exhibited itself in a variety of ways, none of them violent. His potty mouth was nothing new, but his verbal outbursts became increasingly petulant and childish, like accusing Mom of caring more about Raymond and me than him. His whining demands were like an adolescent regression he dished out on a daily basis. Mom felt like a 24/7 on-demand mother. Giv-ing, getting, buying, feeding, clothing, kissing boo-boos—for my father!

The slide into dysfunction is usually just that; not something that happens overnight, but more of an invasive, malignant, creep-ing vine that takes root and silently takes over. While there was plenty of dysfunction from the very beginning, Mom came to real-ize that somewhere along the way they had crossed a line.

She could not say exactly when it was or where—although she wondered if my father might have the intellectual capability to take the whole mess apart and sort it out in a way that had escaped her. He was smart, and he was rightfully proud of his sergeant status in the crime scene investigation unit at the NYPD. He had worked hard, studied, and had kept his eye on the prize since starting his career in law enforcement. But something along the way had gone terribly awry for them to be in the car, idling at a red light when my father, as though he were thinking aloud quietly said, "Can you imagine how it feels to have to tell a mother that her child is dead? I have seen so many murders that I could probably shoot you and make it look like a stranger did it." Then at the sound of her startled cry, he blinked, chuckled and said, "Oh, just kidding."

Mom could not figure out where his new affinity for threatening and testing violent theories on her was coming from. After more than seven years on the force, she suspected—*hoped*—that the interrogation tactics he used to perform his job had simply become so ingrained in him he could confuse a conversation between himself and a suspect, with a conversation with his wife. He had the ability to manipulate people; he was trained to lie and tell stories to get a suspect to confess. He had begun telling Mom about other cops who, according to my father, got away with murdering their wives because of their law enforcement background. Their marriage had always been troubled, she knew that, but to suggest he could kill her and get away with it was entering a whole new level of dysfunction—and she was desperate to believe that he wasn't serious or capable of committing such a deed.

There was no easy way to broach this subject with him, but she realized she had no choice. The best approach she could think of was to prepare a delicious meal and then try to engage him in a civilized discussion after Raymond and I had gone to bed. He loved red sauce, so she began cooking it early in the day. Raymond's basketball team that my father coached had a game that day, and even though they won, my father screamed at Raymond for not playing well. Then, as always, he turned on Mom. When we got home, Raymond and I went to our rooms. We had lost our appetites.

Mom told me that she had to follow through with her plan of talking to him, even after the scene in the car. After she put my father's food in front of him and sat down at the table she said, "Ray, I need to talk to you." She said she tried to keep her voice steady while her stomach churned. "When you say stuff to me like, 'I know how to kill you,' or 'accidents' happen, I get scared, truly terrified."

"You're overreacting, Barbara. I'm trying to eat."

"I understand you might not want to talk about it, Ray, but we can't have you acting like this, especially around the children. They can understand what you're saying, you know?"

"And how do I act, Barbara?"

She could tell he was baiting her. She didn't want to argue with him, but she felt she had no choice. This was important enough not to back down.

"Like a monster, that's how. Yelling all the time, making threats, telling me you know how to make me disappear! It's not right, Ray."

"It's not my problem you can't take a joke." He was standing now, pacing back and forth beside the table. He stopped and looked straight at her. His eyes twitched a bit. Mom said she couldn't breathe. His words came in beats: "You're. Calling me. Crazy. ARE YOU?"

He was gnawing on his bottom lip, much as he would right before he started screaming obscenities at drivers who irritated him.

"Ray, I'm just concerned." She rushed the words out and might have raced out the door if it weren't for us—she would have never left Raymond and me behind. "I want you to be happy, and clearly you're not. Nobody is."

He disappeared from her line of vision. She told herself to turn around to look at him, but she couldn't.

"You don't know what unhappy is. I will show you unhappy!" he screamed into her ear. "You idiot! You good-for-nothing bitch!"

Scalding liquid showered over her shoulders and ran down her arms. The acidic tomato sauce splattered in hot chunks that oddly resulted in a rush of feverish chills and then merciful numbness as another wave of red juice was tossed from the pot and onto the rest of her body. "Goddamn. Bullshit!"

His cursing was a sign that it was over. She was right about that because he stormed out of the house. She saw the mess on the floor and thought that he wouldn't like that, and she'd better clean it up. Most likely, her "calm" stemmed from shock, and when she stood up, she saw spots of green, purple and black, and thought she might faint. But she thought that she couldn't do that—she needed to clean up the mess.

Between baby steps and lurches, she made it to the pantry. Once there she leaned against it for support until her knees buckled and she slid to the floor. The enormity of what had just happened hit her and she began to cry.

Then she saw Raymond, silently standing in the doorway.

Raymond's Memories

A memory I have was after one of my basketball games when I was about 8 or 9 years old. I had not played very well, but still, we had won the game.

In the car on the way home, my father immediately began to scream at me. He said that I was an embarrassment to him and called me a waste of his time. He then shifted his attention to my mom, saying that it was her fault I was like this. He told her she was the reason I embarrass him because I am weak like her and will be a nothing, like her. He blamed her for everything and this continued in the car until we got home.

I remember that when we got home, my sister and I immediately went upstairs to get away from him—we couldn't stand listening to him anymore. I waited until I heard the door slam downstairs and I knew he was finally gone. At that point I went downstairs and when I got down there, I looked into the kitchen and saw my mom sitting on the floor of the kitchen crying hysterically with the pasta sauce she was making for dinner all over her. She told me to go upstairs, please, and that everything was okay.

It is still a memory that disturbs me and gives me nightmares to this day. I will remember what I saw when I looked into that kitchen until the day I die.

CHAPTER EIGHT

The Monster Is Loose

"We gain strength, and courage, and confidence by each experience in which we really stop to look fear in the face . . . we must do that which we think we cannot."
—ELEANOR ROOSEVELT

According to *Webster's Dictionary,* a liar is "a person who knowingly utters falsehood; one who declares to another as a fact what he knows to be not true, and with an intention to deceive him." When my mom considered the ramifications of seeking treatment after being scalded by the red sauce my father had thrown on her, she knew she was going to have to lie about it to protect those she loved—but that was far from an intention to deceive. It was obvious to her that my father didn't love her. Now that the monster had revealed himself, she wondered if he had the ability to love anyone at all—including Raymond and me. This meant she had to love us enough for two parents and she had to keep us safe from any potential backlash—of which there could be plenty if my father had reason to think she turned him in to the authorities. He was one of *them,* and they protected their own, as he had repeatedly drilled into our heads.

Mom knew that she could not tell the truth of what had happened to her. It would be another secret—like her not telling anyone about the crime videos or photos. If she told anyone about that, she wasn't sure what he could do to her that was worse than what he had already done, but he was clearly capable of the unthinkable. She couldn't risk his unhinged wrath, and she would not jeopardize Raymond and me more than we had already been damaged. She worried how Raymond was ever going to forget the sight of her in that state. He had not watched our father throw the scalding sauce on her, but just witnessing the aftermath was destructive enough. She realized that she was probably in a state of shock—not just from the pain that was replacing the numbness, but from the inconceivable physical, mental and emotional trauma. Her skin was badly burned in patches where her clothes hadn't protected her. She had to seek treatment, and there was only one person she could go to. By this time my father had returned and had gone upstairs to their bedroom without even checking on her.

She walked into their bedroom and told him that she needed to go to the hospital. His response was to glare at her and say, "Why did you make me do this to you?"

She had some questions for him: *Why did you do this to me? How could you do it?* But of course she didn't dare ask them. He was smart enough to do this heinous thing and not only get by with it, but make her wonder exactly what she had done to set him off so she would be sure not to do it again.

He then made it clear to her how cunning the monster that lived inside him could be now that a vicious act of violence had released him: "While you are at the hospital, I want you to remember that I am here with your children alone. You'd like to see them safe in their beds when you get home, right? If I see a cop car so much as ride by this house, Barbara, I will know you told."

Mom knew that my father didn't bluff. She drove herself to the nearest clinic. She hadn't been able to think clearly enough to make up a story to tell, so when the emergency-care nurse asked what happened, she said the first thing that popped into her head—that she had dropped a pot of boiling water on herself. The nurse bought the excuse, or at least she didn't pursue the possibility that Mom had just told a lie.

Her whole life was a lie, but she knew better than to tell the truth. Oprah could have all the experts in the world on her show, but Mom didn't think anyone but other women who were trapped as she was truly understood what a slow, seductive process abuse could be. The abuser is patient in his progression while the abused suckers herself into believing her own lies—until there is an exponential escalation of violence and she is drenched in boiling hot red sauce. Once things got to this point, there were no choices if she wanted to remain alive—or, more important to Mom, that Raymond and I would survive this horror.

She woke up to pain and bandaged arms the next morning. My father was gone and she didn't know where he was. Mom, Raymond and I went to Nanni's house, and Aunt Robin was there.

"Barbara! What in God's name happened to your arms?" Aunt Robin pointed to the white gauze peeking out from the cuff of the long-sleeved sweater Mom had worn to camouflage the evidence.

Nanni touched her other arm and looked at her the way only a mother could, as if she knew the bandages were the least of the problem.

"I knocked over a pot of boiling water yesterday while making macaroni. I'm such a klutz!" Mom knew she had to get out of there and she had to do it quickly before she broke down. She told Nanni that she needed to run some errands and asked if she could watch Raymond and me for about an hour.

Aunt Robin told her that she would go with her, even though Mom tried to talk her out of it.

As I have heard the story from Mom, she drove to the dry cleaners, pretending to check on a skirt of mine that she had left there the day before and knew perfectly well it wouldn't be ready yet. The clerk reminded her that it wouldn't be ready for a few more days, along with a look that suggested she wasn't all there or that perhaps something must not be right with her world. Her apology and forced smile were automatic, and she returned to the car, dreading the confrontation from Aunt Robin.

"Hey, look at me. What are you doing?"

"Going to the meat market." Mom couldn't look at her, she didn't dare. She put the car into gear and started driving . . . somewhere; she couldn't remember where the meat market was.

Aunt Robin was having none of it. "You did not burn your arms with a pot of water and don't waste your breath trying to convince me that's what actually happened. Something is going on that you can't just cover up with a sweater. What did he do to you?"

Aunt Robin was determined to get it out into the open, and Mom was just as determined to refuse the listening ear she so desperately needed. It was more than my father telling her to keep her mouth shut; it was a primal instinct for self-preservation. Mom knew that Aunt Robin wouldn't hesitate to blow the whistle on my father, and there was no way to make anyone understand what even Mom hadn't understood until now—there was no reasoning with a monster. She wasn't dealing with a person whose ethics and morals and sense of right and wrong were guided by the same principles that she and most of humanity abided by.

Then Mom was stuck by a startling and highly disturbing possibility. Was it possible that my father might relate on some level to those he pursued? Could that be part of what made him so good at his job—the ability to get into the heads of the perverts and perpetrators because his own head was wired that way? She had seen too many pictures and videos of what those people—not people, *monsters*—were capable of, and after last night she couldn't dispute the hard evidence that he was quite possibly among those who didn't have a normal conscience to guide them.

Mom pulled over to the side of the road and looked at Aunt Robin—sister to sister, woman to woman. Her eyes said what she couldn't: *Please let's not talk about it. I'm begging you.* Then she said, "Robin, just keep me company."

They drove around Howard Beach, past their grammar school; the church Aunt Robin got married in; the McDonald's where Mom used to hang out with Annie and the gang in high school.

Before she knew it, they were heading over the causeway to the neighboring town of Ozone Park. As the car turned off Woodhaven Boulevard, she gently let up on the accelerator.

Aunt Robin peered out of her window and asked Mom where she was going.

Mom said, "A place where I can never go back." Mom wondered if she'd had some subconscious need to torture herself with
what might have been and could never be. The car crept past a
driveway paved with blacktop that led to a garage in which she
had once been passionately kissed. She was barely past the house
when the door swung open. Johnny Dee moved toward the street
with the same determined strut he had back in high school. He
retrieved the big trashcan that her car had bunted to the sidewalk
then turned abruptly in search for the lid, oblivious to the crawl-
ing vehicle and Mom's stare from the rearview mirror. Mom said
he looked casual and cute in a white T-shirt and gray sweatpants
that made it obvious he had taken good care of himself over the
years. She wondered if he was still living with his parents or just
visiting. Whatever the reason, he materialized in that exact
moment, and she was torn between gratitude for even a glimpse at
what happiness had once looked like, and deep regret that she had
encountered this blatant reminder of it.

Mom had made her bed with a man whom she never should
have married—a man who had transformed from an ambitious
young cop into some strange and dangerous creature she didn't
recognize as completely human.

She heard years later that Johnny Dee had married. As much as
she would like to have closure on that chapter of her life, Mom has
put it behind her.

Even though there were many times that Raymond and I witnessed our father abusing Mom, there were even more that we

didn't. We had learned at a very young age to stay in our rooms when our father got angry. Unlike most kids, we never argued when Mom told us to go to bed early. She described the following as one of those times:

The slap was like so many that had gone before—she saw it coming but there was nothing she could do to prevent it. She was trying to breathe, but couldn't get enough air through her nostrils. She opened her mouth to breathe, and she tasted the remnants of cheese doodles from the couch cushions. The cheese doodles must have been what she was being punished for. It was always guesswork as to what she had done wrong, and just in case this was a double-slap infraction, she kept her face buried in the cushion.

He used to stay away from her face and the places she couldn't hide with her clothes, but after the red sauce incident he seemed to have lost what little self-control he had, whether it was a slap, a kick, a punch or, if she was lucky, he would just spit on her. It had taken years to escalate to the scalding, and in an odd way, it seemed almost like regression to revert to pinching and punching after something so over the top—as if cruelty could be measured.

When Mom felt it was safe to sit up, she saw that he was on his knees beside the couch rocking back and forth making whimpering sounds. Then something totally unexpected happened; he pressed his face into her lap. He kept rocking, harder and faster, his whimpers turning to muffled cries of "Mama. Mama."

Mom didn't know what to think. She asked him if he was okay. She knew he was drunk, which was why she had sent us to bed early and told us to close our doors, but this was something extraordinarily strange.

"I love you, Mama. Please, not the belt. Mama . . . Mama!"

As much as Mom hated his hitting her and the yelling, at least it was familiar. She had to make this bizarre, freakish behavior stop. Ray, it's me. Barbara. What's wrong?"

"Hold me, Mama! Please Mama, please hold me!"

He continued to cry and hold his arms out to her like a baby, and Mom was desperate to find something that would snap him out of it. My Grandma Edith was very ill by this time, so it was not possible for her to say something like, "We'll go see her tomorrow, Ray." Instead, she tried to quiet him down with soothing words of, "There, there, it will be all right."

"Mama?" Ray asked hopefully.

It was creepy, and even scary. Still, Mom couldn't believe how far she was willing to go. She held him and said, "Yes, Ray, I'm here."

The next morning Mom told us to use the half bath downstairs to get ready for school. She could hear him whistling from the shower above us. It always amazed her how he woke up without an alarm and spent so much time in the bathroom showering, shaving, and doing who knew what else, to get himself ready for wherever he was going that day. She didn't take the chance of knocking on the door to hurry him up so I could get something I needed.

His chipper mood made Mom think that he must not have remembered the scene he made the night before. After assuring him she wasn't going to beat him with a belt or call him names, she had finally gotten him to bed where he passed out in the fetal position, still wearing the slacks and necktie he wore to work that day. He fell asleep sucking his thumb.

What little sleep she got was troubled, and she was awake before dawn to make our breakfast and get us out the door extra early. We were no sooner gone than she heard him come down the stairs, still whistling. She braced herself, certain the whistling was a trap.

"Good morning," he sang gaily, while making a beeline to the coffee pot.

Watching him devour his eggs nauseated her.

Mom said that the yellow roses that arrived that day at work did nothing to soothe her queasy stomach. Her co-workers must have noticed by now that Mom didn't have the same delighted reaction to receiving flowers that other women had, but if anyone suspected a dark reason for that, they didn't make it their business.

She didn't get flowers often, but when she did, it was because he was struck with something resembling a conscience. This made her wonder if he did remember the night before. She reluctantly unpinned the envelope from the bow and removed the card. It said, "Hurting you hurts me. I'm sorry. Let's have a wonderful cruise. Ray."

And Mom thought, *Of course—the cruise.*

Nanni and Poppop had decided that for their anniversary they wanted to take a family cruise and had even invited Vincent, Linda, and their daughter, Kathleen. Although the invitation sounded tempting to Mom, she knew it would not be a good idea. While being surrounded by family for a whole week would provide a certain amount of protection, pretending as though nothing was wrong, especially to those closest to her, took a lot out of her, and a cruise meant she would have to be "on" for seven straight days rather than a few hours at a time. However, she thought there might be the possibility that "Vacation Ray," might show up.

Ultimately the decision wasn't hers, because my father was chomping at the bit to get on that ship.

They were no sooner in their room than he started complaining. "This is a small ship, not the new one everyone is talking about. I can't believe your parents cheaped out and didn't get me a balcony."

Mom quickly shut the door. She wasn't sure if it was because his attack was directed at my grandparents and she wasn't going to stand for that, or perhaps she was feeling brave because he was usually careful not to raise suspicions in public and she didn't think he would strike her for asserting herself, but she said, "They didn't have to pay for this trip, but they did. You should tell them thank you, Ray!"

"Are you kidding me? Shut the fuck up before I do it for you."

"Lower your voice."

"Your father should do more for me, especially for putting up with you!" This wasn't the first time he had attacked my grandfather. Mom couldn't figure out why he disliked him so—not that he needed a reason to fly into a rage about anything or bad mouth anyone. What concerned her most was that he wasn't showing his typical care in putting up a front when someone could surely hear him through the thin walls.

"I work so hard, I deserve a free trip . . . and a better one than this poor excuse for a cruise line. I'll have to sit around a kiddie pool with your pompous brother and his pain in the ass wife and your stupid sister and pretend to want to be here! This is no vacation. This sucks!"

"Well, if you hate them so much, you can at least hang out with your brother. Don't forget it was my father's idea to invite him and Linda. Can't you at least give him credit for that?"

"Please, like I want to be caught dead in public with my brother. Vincent is such a slob and his wife is no better. It makes me sick how fat they are. Just like you, you low-life fatty. A good-for-nothin' fatty with a good-for-nothin' family."

Mom couldn't understand how anyone could spew such hatred in private, then turn around and be such a phony in public. She also told me that my father's hatred for Vincent and Linda stemmed from the fact that he was insanely jealous of them because they had more money than we did. I saw this myself. He was obsessed with constantly trying to do better than they did.

It was while Mom and Aunt Robin were walking the deck around the perimeter of the ship that she confronted Mom again. "What are you doing? When are you going to leave him?" By this point, Mom wasn't going to insult her intelligence any longer.

"It's not that simple, Robin." She knew this sounded like a hollow answer because it wasn't too long ago that Aunt Robin had ended her own marriage. Only their circumstances were different; she had been unhappy, but she hadn't been married to a sick person who made dangerous threats about hurting her loved ones and having no remorse for the injuries he inflicted on her. My father was a loaded gun, just like the ones he left laying around our house. He went around half-cocked most of the time, and there was no telling when or why he might go off, or who might be hit next.

"You can tell yourself that, Barbara, but don't try to tell it to me." Robin squeezed her hand. "When you're ready, let me know. I'll be here."

Robin Catanzarite, Barbara's sister:
At first, I thought Ray was a nice guy who came from a decent family. But when they were engaged, I remember him as being controlling. He always wanted to know where Barbara was going, who she was with, and when she was coming back. I thought it was just a matter of his being controlling, but I came to realize it was more than that. As time went on, he was more outspoken and confrontational with not only Barbara, but others in the family as well.

Over the years, I was more and more uneasy in Ray's company. He made almost everyone uneasy: when he acted like he was better than others; when he came late to family gatherings, acting agitated and didn't offer an explanation; when he thought he knew everything; when he put other people down; when he blamed Barbara if something went wrong; when he spoke in a disrespectful manner to my parents; when he treated small children or animals badly.

I remember an occasion at a bowling alley on Raymond's birthday when Ray said to a little boy, "Get out of here you little f-ing jerk." I was standing next to another boy's mother. She said she couldn't believe he would speak to a little kid like that, and she thought he was horrible and cruel.

There wasn't much to like about Ray. He was condescending and didn't even try to endear himself to anyone nor would he go out of his way for anyone. He treated people as though they were beneath him.

Holidays were never easy with Ray. He wanted Barbara to make dinner and have people at his house, but he never wanted to visit anyone else. He was always annoyed about something, which made others extremely uncomfortable. If things were not perfect (as he wanted them), everyone knew about it because of the way he acted. There were a few times when it seemed he was actually trying to make the day miserable for his family.

Ray seemed proud when Jennifer was born, but he quickly lost interest in her. He thought Barbara should always be the one to change the baby and take care of her. He didn't want anyone (specifically our mom) to help take care of the baby—he thought Barbara should be the one to do everything.

There were many times when I was with Barbara that she seemed unhappy. When I lived next door to her, I saw her crying on several occasions. I always assumed they had an argument and she was upset. I didn't know how truly horrible her life was in the house right next door!

She was always nervous when we were together and Ray wasn't around. She would have to answer his phone calls—sometimes ten or twelve over the course of a few hours. Barbara spent less and less time with me as the years went on.

The few occasions when Mike and I went out with Barbara and Ray, she didn't seem comfortable with our being together. He would drink and embarrass her, talk down to her and was cruel.

Barbara would say things like, "Ray will kill me if I don't get home," or "Ray doesn't want me to go to dinner with my friends from work," or "Ray said I don't need those people I work with." All these things made her unhappy.

Jennifer and Raymond are very special to me, but whenever I asked to take them places when they were little, Barbara would say, "Ray and I will go too." I couldn't understand why she wouldn't want me to take the kids places by myself.

The kids were unhappy all the time. Jennifer and Raymond grew more and more withdrawn as they got older. Raymond didn't talk much to anyone—he didn't look directly at us when we were speaking to him.

Both kids noticeably ignored Ray. They would walk into a room and kiss everyone except him. They looked at their father in complete disgust when he was speaking loudly and trying to command the attention of everyone in the room.

When Jennifer seemed unhappy, I asked her if there was something wrong or anything she wanted to talk about—she always said everything was okay. At one point, she lost a lot of weight and I wrote her a note asking her if she was okay, and she said everything was fine. I guess I knew that something was wrong, but didn't know if it was my place to interfere.

Raymond appeared to be embarrassed by Ray—especially if he was with friends or teammates. Ray would tell Jennifer and Raymond that they weren't good at sports or should do better in school, even though they were both great students and excelled at sports. Our family discussed that Ray was fortunate to have such a nice family and such good, intelligent kids. We couldn't understand what would make him so miserable.

Unfortunately, Barbara never confided in me about her life with Ray. I always knew life with him was not easy for her, Jennifer and Raymond, but as the years went on, I realized that there were some major problems in their family. One of Ray and Barbara's friends, who has since passed away, made a comment to me at a party in Barbara and Ray's back yard. He said, "Why does Barbara let him treat her that way?"

I don't recall what I felt when I heard that Ray was dead. I think I was in shock that this happened. I was thankful that it wasn't my sister or her children who were dead. I don't remember what I said to Jennifer and Raymond—I know I wanted to reassure them that I loved them and that we would come together as a family and get through this.

I worry that Jennifer and Raymond might think I could have or should have done more to help them.

I worry that they might think they don't have support from the rest of the family.

I worry that if their mother has to go away, they will think that they don't have a "home," or anyone who loves them.

I worry that they won't be able to put this behind them and they will carry this burden for the rest of their lives.

I worry that they might feel embarrassment or shame because of their father.

I worry that they don't know how much they mean to me or how much their mother means to me!

I have asked God why Barbara and her children had to endure such pain and suffering; I asked God why He didn't open my eyes to what was going on; I asked God why I wasn't given the chance to help them. But now I have asked God to help Barbara , Jennifer and Raymond overcome the horror they lived and move forward with their lives.

CHAPTER NINE

The Sheehan Family Lie

"Lying is done with words and also with silence."
—ADRIENNE RICH

Mom's mind ran through all the possible scenarios of how she could leave my father and end the escalating emotional and physical abuse. Once she figured out the first and hardest part—how to leave him—then she could go back to work fulltime, move in with my grandparents until she found an apartment or maybe he would agree to let her keep the house until Raymond and I were both over eighteen. She knew that was wishful thinking.

Yet there might be something—she wondered to what extent he was cheating on her. Not that she cared if he wanted to be intimate with someone and not with her; after all the abuse she had received from his hands, she couldn't bear the thought of his touching her—something he had not done since she had conceived Raymond. She could hope that the cheating might be a bargaining chip she could use to get all of us free of him.

The problem was gathering the concrete proof of his infidelity, since the evidence she had was circumstantial and too easily blamed on his devotion to his job. The devotion she didn't doubt, but she had been married to a detective long enough to know there was usually time to come home and sleep, if only for a short time, clean up and change clothes on a daily basis. Yet he was often out for days and nights on end, and she didn't dare question his where-abouts—or risk the reprieve we all enjoyed when he was gone.

Another part of the problem was that even if she caught him in the act, it could still be next to impossible to convince him to let her leave him and take Raymond and me with her. He was crystal clear concerning his stance on divorce. However, if Mom could somehow convince him to agree to a trial separation, she could begin to establish a life independent of his. Then, safely out of his reach, she could work her way to the ultimate freedom of divorce. That was the goal, but always, always it came back to how to get away without his coming after us. That's what had prevented her from packing us into the car and running away years ago. He was a detective, and he had considerable means at his disposal to track her down—he had been sure to tell her time and time again that his training and resources would allow him to find all of us, wher-ever we were. And when he did—just the thought of it gave her chills.

She then thought about offering to let him have everything. She could tell him that he could keep all his money and use it to vacation in style. She could then make a new start with whatever assistance my grandparents could give her with Raymond and me while she got on her feet. Aunt Robin had scarcely an idea of the extent of his abuse and Nanni and Poppop had even less. She would need to keep it that way until he was no longer a threat, although that could be indefinitely. She knew they would help her in any way they could once she got her foot in their door. There was only one way to find out if it might work.

She gathered all the courage she had and broached the subject shortly after returning from the family cruise. His response to her well-rehearsed suggestion fell worse than flat.

He yelled down the hall to us from their bedroom door, "Did you hear that, kids? Your mother wants to leave you." At first I thought, *Why would my mom leave me and Raymond—and especially leave us with HIM?* But then I realized that he was once again making something up to blame my mother for, or make it look like she was the uncaring one. My brother and I both knew that she would never leave us. If she wanted to, she would have years ago—she would have left the abuse my father was putting her through. We knew she loved us way too much to leave us. She always told us we didn't have to worry, because she would always be there for us.

Mom told me that she had to keep us out of it. She knew that we were afraid of him, but that was even more reason that she couldn't let this drop. She told him that maybe they needed a break, a trial separation, and that it would be good for both of them, and especially for him. She then appealed to his self-centered, greedy nature and told him that instead of his money going to support the three of us, he could get a sports car, and go on all the vacations he wanted. She didn't get to finish before he cut her off.

"Oh, no, you're not feeding me that shit. How stupid do you think I am, Barbara? You say it's a trial separation and you take off. Then the next thing I know it's divorce papers—along with wanting everything you can get your greedy hands on."

"Look, Ray, all I'll ask for is my car."

"See? You're already thinking about getting a divorce. How long have you been thinking about it, huh? *Huh?*"

He was in her face now, and although she was scared, she was used to being hit. Just getting this far in the conversation gave her courage to continue. She assured him that she didn't want a divorce; she wanted to work things out but felt they could do it better apart than together. She had to say that to be able to take the first step and get us out of the house.

He didn't say anything so she rushed on. "I can take the kids and stay at my parents' house while you have a chance to live life on your own terms. You never got to do that, getting married so young—always working so hard to keep a roof over our heads instead of spending money on the stuff you really want. Like cars and vacations?"

She was repeating herself, but still he didn't say anything. She thought it was an answer to prayer, but just to be sure, she said, "Okay?"

His response was a "pfft" and a hand gesture of dismissal, and then he turned his back to her and walked away. Mom was careful not to let on how happy she was as she went down the stairs to the kitchen. He hadn't followed her, but it was still too early to celebrate. She knew that she still had to get on her feet while he became so enamored with the single life he wouldn't want her back. Still, this was a very big head start in that direction, and according to Mom, what had been most important was that she could finally give Raymond and me a life that wasn't filled with dysfunction, violence, and fear.

The three of us were sitting at the kitchen table eating peanut butter out of the jar with spoons. I guess Mom was in such a state of euphoria over asserting herself and the thought that we were about to be free, she just wanted to do something fun with us. But I also think she was probably using the time to work out the plans of actually leaving, and thinking about how difficult it was going to be to tell my grandparents why she had to do this. Maybe this is the reason she chose to call Nanni and Poppop to let them know we were coming instead of grabbing us, still in our pajamas, and getting out while she could.

Just as she lifted the receiver from the kitchen phone, we heard what sounded like thunder coming from upstairs. We were paralyzed with fear, knowing that it was my father coming down the stairs.

He loomed in the kitchen doorway, in a rage. "You have no college education, haven't had a real job in years, and your friends all dumped you. Like it or not, you need me, Barbara. And I'll be damned if you're taking those kids to live with your father so he can turn them into shanty dumbasses like he did you! Now give me that!"

He grabbed the phone from my mom's hands and then repeatedly beat her with the receiver. He pounded the back of her head yelling, "You're going nowhere, bitch!" She covered her head as best as she could with her forearms and cowered down, elbows on the floor. That gave him better access to her back, and when he tired of beating her, he dropped the phone and kicked her in the ribs.

Raymond and I were crying, terrified. We shouted and pleaded with him to stop, and told him that we wouldn't go anywhere.

He shouted back at us, "Your mother is a good for nothing

piece of shit!" and he kicked her again. "She's useless! I feel bad for you that you have her for a mother. Now get upstairs or I'll hit her until you do!"

We had no choice—we were afraid he would kill her if we didn't. Mom said she was so afraid he might go after us next that she mustered up the strength to get on her hands and knees, and then staggered to her feet. She had barely straightened out when he punched her in the face. As she felt her left eye swell, he hit her again, in her right eye.

Blood was obscuring her vision, but she could hear him loud and clear as he said calmly, "If you tell anyone what just happened or *ever* try to leave this marriage again, I will invite your father to lunch and then gut him like a fish while he's eating a ham sandwich. I'll dump him where they'll never find him. I'm just looking for a reason to get him. Go ahead, Barb. *His* blood will be on *your* hands the next time you try to pull something like this."

Mom didn't have to wonder if he would do such a hideous thing—she knew he would.

My first memory of my father abusing my mother was when I was four years old. I was in my bed, just about to go to sleep when I heard dad breaking things—yelling and screaming at Mom.

For as long as I can remember, I was afraid of my father—afraid of what he would do next, and especially afraid that he would kill my mother. There wasn't a day that I wasn't afraid he would shoot her. He would pick up one of his guns whenever he was angry— and they were always close by. We could hear him slapping her, beating her, screaming at her and throwing things. We were stuck in our rooms forced to listen to this, and weren't able to do anything about it except pray.

Mom cutting their engagement cake

Our parents on their
wedding day

Mom on their honeymoon

Mom on our parents' second anniversary

Mom and me when I was a toddler

Baby Raymond and me

Raymond and me one Easter

Our family on vacation

My mom and me

My husband, Jesse, and me

Raymond and his fiancée, Shannon

The three of us at my wedding

I would sit in my room and cry and pray and shake. Sometimes Raymond, who is three and a half years younger than I am, would come in my room and try to comfort me. He would say that it would be okay. In the mornings, we were both silent. We didn't discuss the "events."

I remember a particularly disturbing incident when I was a freshman in high school. I was in my room and could hear the sound of his hitting her in their bedroom. I started screaming and crying for him to stop, and he came out of their room laughing. What could possibly have been funny? I'll never understand . . .

Mom wouldn't say anything back to him, but Raymond and I were never angry with her for that—we knew it would only make things worse. We couldn't even hug her or kiss her if he was around.

I was twelve years old and we were at a professional baseball game. My father choked and someone performed the Heimlich maneuver. My father was grateful. I wasn't. I couldn't understand why someone would help him; why they would want to save this horrible man's life?

I often thought about stabbing him when he was sleeping. One night when I was in the eighth grade, he had been in one of his crazy moods, abusing Mom. After he left the house I held a knife in my hand and cried. I used to pray that he would be hit by a car and be killed. It never crossed my mind that Mom would kill him, but it is the best thing that could have happened. People have speculated since the shooting that she could have, should have gotten out. Mom, Raymond, and I are the only people alive who knew what went on in that house. The only choice she had was death—and very possibly not only her own.

Raymond's Memories

My first memory of my dad abusing my mom was from an incident I witnessed when I was about four years old: I was playing with a basketball outside. My parents were also outside and my dad was mad about something. He was yelling, screaming, and cursing at my mom. She was holding some keys for some reason and he tackled her to the ground, then left.

We always walked on eggshells, so afraid we would set him off and he would take it out on Mom—although he didn't seem to need an excuse. Any time we were in the car, no matter what happened—if there was traffic, it was my mom's fault; a car cutting him off was my mom's fault; and once when we were driving Upstate and the E-Z pass wasn't in the car, he back-handed her across the face because it was her fault it wasn't there. There was always the verbal abuse: waste-of-life; you'll never be anything; you've ruined my life; fat, useless, cunt; bitch; fat ass. Often, the name-calling would escalate to hitting her, and then he would leave. We never knew where he went.

Jen and I were both afraid of him. That never changed —for either of us.

Barbara Henry, Barbara' mother:
We first knew Ray's brother Dan. He was a deacon in our church and an okay guy. He became pretty friendly with us. We saw a lot of him, but he never spoke too highly of his family or of their home life.

We met the rest of the family at Dan's ordination into the priest-hood. Ray's dad seemed like a fine man, but his mother was very demanding and envious of other people, including her own family. She hated Howard Beach and always told Raymond and Jennifer, "Here comes your young grandma," in reference to me. She was not a nice person. Ray's twin brother, Vincent, said one day, "I don't know why my brother does these things. We lived our lives like this at home with our own mother."

At first, Ray seemed okay when he and Barbara were dating. I became a little concerned when he would tell stories of how he and his twin brother and two friends would go on the roof of the apartment house next door and throw cats off just to see them die. I thought this was a terrible "game."

Ray started showing signs of dominance when they were engaged, saying things like, "Where were you?" "Where are you going?" "Why did you do that?" We were always uneasy in his presence—always having to think of what to say and weigh our words before speaking to him. There was nothing to like about him.

When our grandchildren were born, I asked Barbara to call us when she and Ray were going to the hospital so we could go with them. She called and I rode in the car with them and her father followed behind in our car. All Ray did was yell and tell her to stop crying, saying that she was "not in pain."

Holidays were very difficult, from what I saw. He was always yelling, being nasty, never satisfied, always jealous of others. He told Raymond when our second grandson was born, "That's the end of you, Raymond, they will always like him better and love him more than you"—which was totally untrue!

Barbara and the kids were never happy. We always worried about them. My nephews said they never knew young Raymond could speak until after his father was gone. He was quiet and never spoke much prior to his father dying.

I always sensed something was wrong. I asked Barbara many times if everything was okay. She would always say that everything was fine.

But she would say things like, "Please don't say anything to him because you don't know what he will do."

Barbara seldom called when Ray was at home. When he was, I could hear him coughing in the background and she would hang up immediately and not call back for a day or two.

I was surprised when I heard that Ray was dead. I used to think that it might be my daughter this would happen to some day—even Ray's twin brother {Vincent} told us he thought it would be the other way around.

I worry about the abuse that Jennifer and Raymond have suffered. Will they ever be able to overcome all the grief they have endured in their lives? They are beautiful, intelligent, loving adults, and we will always be here for them.

Jennifer came to our house after this tragedy and I told her that we love her and we will always be here for her. My nephew took Jennifer to pick Raymond up at school in Connecticut and to tell him what happened. Both of them have said, "I am very proud of my mom."

I have questioned God. I asked Him why it had to happen like this. "Why didn't you make him leave?" But mostly, I thank Him every day that this did not happen the other way around. We have our daughter and our grandchildren, whom we love very much!

To make sure she didn't fall out of line, my father began a weekly ritual of giving her a play-by-play on how he would kill my grandfather, Raymond and me, her, and then himself if she dared blow the whistle on him and expose their secret. The order was always the same.

Raymond and I hated to go anywhere with him in the car. He was fond of saying that he would "go out in a blaze of glory," and that we had better "behave" and "be better to him" or he would "make it like our family never existed." We didn't doubt for a minute that it was a possibility.

Mom, Raymond and I went on with our activities as if we didn't live in fear every day of our lives. Mom was active at Our Lady of Grace and supported Raymond and me in our sports and anything else we were doing. She played the role of the doting wife of Sergeant Sheehan, accompanying him on obligatory social events and posing in pictures on the vacations that he insisted we take. Even vacations were not happy times, but he would take pictures to show people what a *normal* family we had. The pictures didn't show him hurting Mom.

My father was the mastermind of the Sheehan Family Lie. He was not usually present in either Raymond's life or mine, unless he saw an opportunity to look good in the eyes of the community. He zeroed in on Raymond's participation in sports and became coach of his grammar school basketball team at Our Lady of Grace. This ultimately did not set well with the other parents. They didn't appreciate his coaching tactics of screaming at their young children and playing favorites. Being the coach was supposed to send a message to our community that he was a normal, involved dad, and it incensed him that others didn't appreciate his contributions—especially when he was asked to step aside by the school administrators at Our Lady of Grace.

Raymond's Memories

Although my dad never physically abused me, there was plenty of verbal and emotional abuse. My dad coached my grade school basketball team. He would scream and curse at me, and tell me in front of my friends that I sucked; that I was an embarrassment to him; that I would never be anything; that I was a waste and never listened to him. I never said anything. I didn't know what to say. The other kids and their fathers didn't say anything either. He yelled at my friends too—not as much as at me, but too much for a six-year-old kid over a grade school basketball game. It embarrassed me more for him to yell at them. It was no big deal for him to yell at me—I heard it all the time, but it really bothered me when he did that to my friends.

Of course, if he was upset with me about anything, he took it out on my mom, all the time, every time. We were riding home from a game when I was about eight and he was mad because I hadn't played well. He yelled and screamed at Mom, saying that Jen and I were just like her—that we were following her and we would be wastes of life, just like she was, and it was her fault. Sometimes these rants and horrible outbursts took place at the dinner table.

Prior to my father's mandatory *retirement* from coaching, he made certain to sabotage any relationships Mom tried to cultivate through the school. She had given up on contacting Annie, her friend from high school. She heard through an indirect channel that early in their marriage my father had ordered Annie never to call her. Apparently he was taking steps from the start to isolate Mom from a potential support system. But she wouldn't risk Annie's safety or that of any one else. By association, anyone she got too close to could possibly be placed in jeopardy themselves, so the best she could hope for was some kind of surface social life based on us and our extracurricular activities. But my father didn't even approve of that kind of socialization.

My father was angry and frustrated after his team had lost a game. He was driving home and out of the blue told Mom, "I don't like you talking to that blonde woman. Her son is a crybaby, just like his father. Don't fraternize with the enemy."

"Ray, you can't be serious."

"You should be paying attention to me, not blabbing your fat mouth with all those stupid women."

While steering the wheel with one hand, he raised the other one, turning the back of it as a signal that he'd whack her if she said anything further.

"And, you, mister." He looked in the rearview mirror and snapped his fingers then at Raymond. "You looked like a weakling out there. You know, you embarrass me sometimes with what a baby you can be. You want to play like a sissy all your life?"

"N-no," Raymond managed to answer. He was only ten years old at the time.

The tiny, frightened sound was more than Mom could stand. She turned in her seat and gave Raymond an encouraging smile.

"Stop that! He has to learn." He pulled the car into the driveway, jumped out and slammed the door behind him. Mom and Raymond remained in their seats until she could no longer bear the sound of his stifled weeping, and she thought, *What is wrong with me? What kind of mother would let her child be treated like this?*

Mom said that she hated herself in that moment. The cowardice, the inability to give us even the semblance of a functional home—she wondered how long this could go on before we were too damaged to function normally.

Empowered by that thought, she stalked into the house. "Don't speak to him like that, Ray!"

"It's my team and my son. I can treat them any way I want."

"They're just kids. I won't let you do this to our child."

He raised his fist and this time she taunted him, "Go ahead. Do what you do best."

The last sound she heard was a loud crack. When she came to, he was standing over her. He told her to clean up the blood.

Lori Angelone, friend of the family:

My family came to know Ray Sheehan because my son, Brian, and Ray's son, Raymond, became friends when they were in first grade at Our Lady of Grace School in Howard Beach, New York. Ray was active in the sports program at our school and he eventually became my son's coach in baseball, basketball and hockey. Our families spent a lot of time together and we socialized after games. At first, I thought he was a pretty nice guy. Because of all the teams he coached that my son was on, we saw him often.

I considered Barbara to be one of my best friends. I thought she was a wonderful person and she would do anything for me. She really put herself out for others. I worked when my kids were young, and she didn't. She would take my kids to practices, birthday parties, etc. when I was not able to because I was working. I never even had to ask her—she just offered to do this.

Our sons hung out together all the time. It wasn't until Brian came home and told us that Ray left his gun laying around all over the house with the kids there that we decided we didn't want him to go to Raymond's house anymore.

An incident worth mentioning about Ray was a time when we had a barbeque for some friends on the team. The kids were in the house and the adults were in the yard. Ray had been drinking (he always seemed to drink when we all went out together). He came in the house to use the bathroom. When I went into the house, my daughter, who was probably around seven at the time, had Ray's loaded gun in her hand. He had left it on top of the toilet tank with all the kids in the house.

By the time our relationship with Ray ended, I absolutely despised him. He, for no apparent reason, started to mistreat my son through sports. He would sit him on the bench for whole games and glare at my husband and me. There was just something evil about it. My son was actually a pretty athletic kid who played sports right through college. This came out of the clear blue sky; there was no explanation for his bizarre behavior other than he decided in his twisted mind that it was time to get rid of us.

Barbara at first would apologize for him, "Ray didn't mean it," "Ray is sorry," but eventually we had enough and when Brian was in the fourth grade we took him off Ray's teams. I even went to the head of the parish to complain about his treatment of the kids. He was not just a coach, but at that time he was head of the whole program. He was obsessed with winning even though the kids were so young. He was very hard on them—he would scream and yell, curse at them and showed favoritism without question. He thought he was Red Holzman coaching the New York Knicks. It was ridiculous. He also would hold practices and attend games while he was on duty with the Police Department. He would be so bold as to park the police car in the school-yard and coach games and score games the entire day at the gym on Sundays. This happened many, many times. He just thought he could do whatever he wanted.

Barbara was always extremely nervous and hyper. She talked fast and couldn't stay still. My friendship with the family ended when the boys were in fourth grade, because of Ray's treatment of Brian. I now realize it was surely intentional to get me out of Barbara's life. I'm sure I was too close for his liking.

I didn't ever see any bruises or marks on Barbara, but I have talked to many people such as a butcher in the local store, people in church, parents of friends, etc. since Ray's death who in fact did see bruises, black eyes and so forth.

Jennifer and Raymond were always such nice kids. Raymond was a quiet kid, but very, very nice. There was an incident of Ray's violence that my husband witnessed, which involved his daughter. Jennifer was probably around eleven at the time. My husband, Ray and the kids were returning from a game or practice. Jennifer said something to her father that he apparently didn't like, and without hesitation, he stopped the car, turned around and hit her in the face. My husband was appalled.

Since the friendship ended so many years ago because of our dislike for Ray, we really didn't have any relationship with the family for many, many years. From what I understand, his violence escalated to a brutal level.

I am so happy that Barbara and I have reconnected, and that we are once again great friends.

There was a period of time when my father's voice didn't get above a low roar, and he was more inclined just to raise his hand than actually hit Mom. More likely, it could have been his own skin he was thinking about. Too many visits to the hospital and the doctors might try to get involved even if my mom wasn't talking.

After he broke her nose, there was an increased risk that my grandparents and Aunt Robin would stop buying her excuses for being so accident-prone and would try to intervene. Mom was frantic to make sure that didn't happen, given my father's instability and his constant access to a gun. He had four guns in the house, with two always in close proximity. If he ever decided to act on his threats, Mom knew that a Sunday would be a perfect time to mow them all down. Mom lived for Sundays. The whole extended family would get together for dinner. It had become a cherished ritual, catapulting her into an alternate reality. Mom said it was the favorite part of her life.

Another reason these gatherings were so important to her was that Mom thought we were safer as a group than individually. Also, she didn't think my father would act on his threats as long as his brother was around. He would never say anything bad about his brother Danny, the priest, but he constantly said disparaging things about Vincent and Linda. However, verbally trashing them in private was on a par with "I can say what I want about my family but nobody else better do it." There was some sense of loyalty there, and he never spoke of killing them—just my grandfather and the three of us before doing himself in.

After years of getting together on Sundays and going on various family excursions like Disney World and the cruise, Mom knew that if those interactions suddenly stopped he would blame her as the cause, which would most likely be true. Once he thought there were no more gatherings because she told their secret, there wouldn't be much incentive left for him to keep up the pretext of "one big happy family."

Something else Mom had to consider—she felt sure her family would believe her, but what if Vincent and Linda didn't? Naturally, they would want to believe that my father was incapable of something so horrible. They might think that she was the crazy one or that she had an ulterior motive for making false accusations. Should that happen, their next step would be to alert him in case Mom's family decided to contact the authorities, so he would have a jump-start in protecting his honor and position on the force. He might then call in his favors or perhaps call the authorities himself to see if he could get his delusional wife committed for observation.

Mom wasn't afraid of being committed. On the contrary—she said it would be a relief to unload her burden on a professional. Her fear was that if the last scenario came to pass, Vincent and Linda's best intentions to shield my father could very well be the tipping point of no return.

Therefore, the Sunday gatherings continued and Mom continued to love them. Then one Sunday, even though my father was always late for these gatherings, he was later than usual. Everyone was gathered around the dining room table, and my Uncle Michael, Mom's brother, expressed concern.

Mom said she was sure he would be home any second. Aunt Robin rolled her eyes. She didn't know how bad things were, but she knew Mom counted on her to keep her silence, which she did. However, sometimes it was hard for her to hide her disgust. As for Uncle Michael, if he had known even a small portion of the truth, there was no way he would have asked for my father's safe return during grace.

No sooner had they started passing the food around when he walked through the front door proclaiming, "I bought a new car!"

"What?" Mom couldn't believe it. She knew that they were up to their eyeballs in debt; plus, they had two very decent cars that got them where they needed to go.

"Everyone, come see!"

They all followed him out the door to see his shiny new toy, parked in the driveway.

"Where's the minivan?" Mom looked around for her car.

"I traded it in."

My father beamed and my mom said nothing as the others, or most of them, made the appropriate ooh's and aah's over his new car.

They met back at the table for a second attempt to eat dinner. Seated at the head, my father plopped a heaping spoonful of lukewarm mashed potatoes onto his plate. He looked over at Uncle Michael and said with a smirk, "Now *you're* not the only one with a new car."

Raymond and I had no idea of our father's deviant sexual behavior until we heard it from our attorney, Mr. Dowd. Mom recently described to me what happened after our company left that night and Raymond and I were in bed. It was difficult to hear and more difficult to write. However, the time of keeping family secrets is over—for Mom and for us.

My father got up from the couch where he had fallen asleep from all the wine he drank and food he had eaten, and went upstairs to bed. Mom cleaned the living room, paying extra attention to the water rings that marred the coffee table. My father would have had a fit if he saw them. He was a neat freak, and she was afraid he would take "the mess" out on Raymond and me, since it was probably our soda cans that had made the marks.

Beneath the end table, she saw my father's big gun. While he had gotten better about not leaving them laying around, they were rarely far from his own reach—the big gun on his hip, the small gun on his ankle. If they weren't literally on him, they accompanied him everywhere he went. Watching the game in the living room, he'd take off the big gun to get more comfortable and place it in the middle of the coffee table or on the end table, where he could see it. He went to the corner store, to the school auditorium, to the backyard to do weed work, and into the bathroom armed.

For him to leave it under the end table while he went to bed meant he must have been really out of it. Mom said she handled the gun as if it were a bomb, removing it delicately from its position and holding it as far away as possible as she walked it upstairs and quietly deposited it on the dresser, near the bedroom door.

Before she could turn around and leave, certain that he must be sound asleep, she heard him whimper only a few feet away.

"Change me, Mommy," he demanded. "I made a mess on myself, Mommy. I need a spanking."

When she looked toward where his voice was coming from, she couldn't believe what she saw. He was lying on the floor, trying to ejaculate into a diaper.

He suddenly held the diaper out to her and flapped it around, more a summons than an invitation for her to play along.

"Watch me," he commanded in a high-pitched voice, his words slurred. "This is what I like, and I shouldn't have to hide it anymore. Come play with me!"

Mom had never seen or heard of anything like this. She couldn't think, couldn't speak; tears ran down her cheeks, and she shook her head *no*.

That's when she heard the sound of a gun cocking—not the big one she had put away on the dresser, but he had three others. The one he usually had close by when he went to bed was the little gun, but it was still powerful enough to be deadly. Especially at such close range.

"Watch me, *I said*." From his position on the floor, he pointed the gun up, directly at her face. His voice had dropped an octave and he was crying, although Mom couldn't tell if he was sad or if it was part of the role-play. She couldn't tell much of anything, she was so disoriented.

"Mommy, I'm bad. Tell me I'm a bad boy." He switched from actor to director in the same sentence. First playing the baby, and then teaching her the lines he expected her to repeat with the threat he would shoot her if she didn't. "Tell me!"

"You're a bad boy?" Mom was openly crying at this point as she tried to focus her attention on the corner of the room. She made a mental note to catch any stray dust bunnies before my father did, and she would gladly clean all day and all night if it would just make this obscene thing go away.

His voice a high-pitched whine again, he panted in time to his rhythmic self-strokes, "Watch me! Watch me! Watch me!"

Mom did as she was told. Even after he put the gun down, she obeyed and watched while he ejaculated into the diaper. He handed her the diaper to dispose of its contents once he was finished. Mom couldn't wait for the night to be over, but the next morning the memory refused to retreat as a mere nightmare. Maybe she never went to sleep.

She couldn't get the scene out of her mind no matter how hard she tried. When it happened a second time, with his making her do something even worse than watch and get rid of the diaper, she began experiencing chest pains.

One day while driving me to gymnastics practice, she experienced such pain she thought she was having a heart attack. Angina, high blood pressure, and an anxiety disorder were the culprits according to the new doctor she saw.

"Are you under any sort of extraordinary stress, Barbara?" the doctor asked while looking over the results of her blood work. "I would like to know more about these panic attacks."

Extraordinary stress? She wanted to tell him about the pushes, the shoves, the kicks when she was down, the spitting in her face, the broken eardrum, the black eyes, the numerous choking incidents, the broken nose—all on different charts with different doctors—the emotional abuse to her and especially to Raymond and me. She wanted to tell him about the guns in the house, how my father slept with them and pulled them on her when he was angry. She wanted to tell him about how she'd discovered that he made sure her best girlfriends never call again, how he said he was going to kill her father, her children, then her and himself. She wanted to scream: *My husband sucks his thumb and makes me wipe his butt like a baby and then comes into a diaper.*

"No more stress than anyone else, Doctor."

"Where were you today, Barbara?" my father immediately asked when he finally came home for dinner that evening. "I called the house all day and you never answered."

"I was at the doctor's."

"Where else did you go?" He sounded like a detective, unconcerned about why she would be at the doctor, unless he was somehow implicated in her need to visit one.

Mom scanned her brain for the list of her daily whereabouts, so she could account for why she wasn't home for most of the afternoon.

"I went to drop off some clothes at the dry cleaners and ran to Sears." She hoped that covered everything. "Oh, and I stopped for gas." Okay, now she had it all.

"Let me see your receipts."

"What?"

"You heard me. I don't believe you. Let me see your receipts."

She didn't know why he was especially suspicious, but she had long ago learned not to question his demands or motives. She rummaged through her wallet for the dry cleaner's slip that had the pick-up date printed on it. Next, she scoured the garbage pail for the Sears receipt. After pulling it out and giving it to him, he studied the time stamp on it.

"This says you checked out at three-thirty. What time were you at the doctor's?"

"Two."

"Where's the gas receipt?"

Mom panicked. She had a bad habit of not taking the gas receipt.

"I don't think I have it."

"You don't have it because you're a liar." He came at her and applied enough pressure to her windpipe to let her know he meant business, but not enough to send her back to the doctor who had made her promise to "take it easy."

"From now on, I want all your receipts. You're not to leave this house unless I know why." He then released his hold.

Mom swallowed hard and nodded her head.

"Good." He gave her his most charming smile. "Be sure to get the kids to bed early tonight. I have a new uniform I want you to see."

CHAPTER TEN

The Calm
Before the Storm

*"I think that we're all mentally ill; those of us
outside the asylums only hide it a little better—
and maybe not all that much better, after all."*
—STEPHEN KING

The first time my father paraded around their bedroom wearing his new blue "cops uniform," Mom's reaction was a mixture of shock, repugnance, and confusion. This was weird—even for him. As always, she was wary.

"I look hot!" he informed her as he strutted back and forth in a metallic blue bra and underwear, with a blue police cap that had the words "Hottie Police" plastered on it. "I should go outside and let people see. They should know how hot I am."

She never knew how she was supposed to respond. "Then why don't you?"

"Are you mocking me?"

"Of course not!" She knew better than that.

He gave a curt nod and instructed, "Say 'Officer Sheehan, you are hot.'"

"Officer Sheehan, you are hot."

"Not like that." He then went to the closet and brought something out. It was a whip, and it frightened Mom. He always hurt her, even if he didn't have a weapon, but now he was holding one and she had no idea of the damage he could do to her with it. He cracked it in the air and his voice matched the snap: "Like you mean it!"

"Officer Sheehan! You. Are. *Hot!*"

"That's better."

Note: *During the trial, I didn't hear any of the testimony regarding my father's sexual deviancy because I was not allowed in the courtroom while my mom was testifying. I waited in the hallway. She came out at one point, crying hysterically. She had been accused of writing a letter to one of these diaper-wearing people, asking them to watch my parents do sexual things or to join them. Of course this was not true, and it crushed my Mom. We have no idea where this came from, unless my father wrote the letter in her name.*

Mom had always found my father's covetous nature annoying, but finally something good came out of it—a home computer. By the late nineties, when the media was hyping the potential devastation of the impending Y2K bug, in his typical impulsive fashion he charged a computer on their Visa card. "Everyone has one," he said. "We should know what all the fuss is about."

That computer was, initially at least, a Godsend. Mom compared it to turning on *Sesame Street* for a screaming toddler. It kept my father quiet, distracted, and out of her hair. Initially, the only interest she showed in the computer was when he asked her to think of a name for their AOL account, which they would share.

Although she had no interest in using the computer herself, she thought his attempt to involve her was sweet. This was so unlike him that she expected "the old Ray" to come back with a vengeance at any moment. Yet the moment stretched out to days, weeks, and then more than a month had passed that she didn't get hit, spat on, threatened, called names, or even had to change a *diaper.* He was distracted *and* in a good mood. He continued his erratic hours, stayed "late at the office," or missed dinner to "have a beer with the guys," but Mom was perfectly happy with the arrangement. There was freedom in their new unspoken understanding. He would do what he did with no questions asked, and she would look the other way.

She suspected his outings were somehow tied to the reduction of his perverse bedroom behavior—that perhaps he had found an outlet to appease his deviancy so he could get his fix outside of the house, which suited her fine. With so much interior stress alleviated, Mom began to live what felt like a normal life. She made lunch dates with Nanni and Aunt Robin, and she even got a new job. This time it was a "real" fulltime job with the department of education. Mom had worked at a law office close to our house two days a week from the time I was born. My dad constantly put her down about her piddling little job.

However, not only did he not fight her on this new job, much to her amazement, he even expressed his appreciation for the monetary contribution she was making to the family pot. As a middle school secretary, she wasn't pulling in what he was making at top pay with the NYPD, but she was able to help pay off their credit card bills, support his impulse buying, and make car payments on trade-ups when he decided he was tired of the *old* car. Mom didn't care if that's where a large chunk of her paycheck went. She was out of the house and earning her own terrific benefits, not the least of which was a growing sense of self-empowerment in the workplace, which translated into more confidence at home.

If he noticed, cared or thought she was getting "too uppity," he made no comment. He was back to good old "Vacation Ray." All of us flourished in this grace period. Mom was able to make friends who had no idea who her husband was. Friends like Betsey, who would become an adult version of Annie—someone she could count on. Behind the desk where she performed her administrative duties, she could almost forget the past and practice being a much better version of the deeply damaged woman she had been.

Time passed quickly, and then for a moment, it stopped. When the tragedy of 9/11 struck, my father was there. I asked God why nice people died and He didn't take my father instead. He was different for a while; just as so many other people were at that time. The brotherhood of first responders, especially cops and firefighters, was celebrated, and we were even closer to being a *normal* family—and it gave my mom hope that even amid tragedy, miracles can happen.

Less than a year after 9/11, my father retired from the force and took a job in the security business. On weekdays, Mom and Dad went to work and Raymond and I went to school. On weekends, Mom cheered Raymond on from the sidelines of his football games. Even then, he was a talented athlete.

Perhaps one of the first signs that my father was reverting to his former self came when Raymond played high school football. He yelled at him from the stands, criticizing his performance. Raymond, however, had been particular in his choice of sports. Football wasn't our father's game. His knowledge was too limited to go up against the coaches or enable him to bully Raymond, who understood the game far better than he did.

This, no doubt, frustrated him, along with the constant reminder that he was no longer the hotshot detective he had considered himself to be at the NYPD. Working as head of security at a financial institution didn't elicit the same sort of respect that was given an officer with the power to flash a badge. In corresponding measure to the lack of respect, his temper got shorter. As his temper got shorter, my weight diminished.

I went to Molloy, a college in the area, so I could live at home. I was in a serious relationship with my boyfriend, Jesse, and I wanted to get on with my life and move away; but I was afraid to leave—afraid of what my dad would do to Mom. I had an eating disorder, anorexia, when I was in college. I just stopped eating and weighed 79 pounds. I saw a social worker at the college for a year, and came to realize that my not eating was the only thing in my life that I could control.

I told the social worker that my dad was violent, but I didn't go into details. She gave me some brochures on domestic violence and told me to give them to my mom. She said. "It's up to her if she wants to leave." I never told her that I didn't give them to my mom. I was afraid my dad would see them and kill her.

Raymond's Memories

Our father treated Jen much worse than he treated me. According to him, everything she said was wrong and she didn't know what she was talking about—something as simple as Jen's saying at the dinner table one night that it was cold out, and he said, "No it's not!" He would hit her, throw her, or come after her—run after her. One time after hitting her while she lay on her bed, he broke the door to her room. Another time when he was mad at her, he grabbed the money she was saving for a trip to Hawaii and threw it on the floor. Mom tried to stop him and he threw her on the floor. He didn't take the money; he was just mad and told Jen that she shouldn't even go.

He seldom asked about our day at school. If he did, whatever we told him was never good enough—such as the time Jen told him that she made a 95 on her report card and he was mad—it had to be 100. Jen was upset because she had done her best and thought she was doing well. Sometimes he ignored us completely. We would come home from school or sports and he could be sitting right there, on the couch, but he wouldn't even look up and acknowledge us. As I got older, I would text Mom to see what kind of a mood he was in so I would know what to expect when I got home.

My mom made me feel good about myself. I was a high school cheerleader and a competitive gymnast. She told me that she loved to watch my routines, whether on the beam or on the floor; that she was in awe of my elastic body and that I moved with the grace of a swan. Her words to me were like giving water to a person who is literally dying of thirst. In contrast, my father had never taken any real interest in my gymnastics or cheerleading, but his earlier indifference transitioned into an outlet for his frustration and he verbally beat on me as he had Raymond when he played basketball in grade school

"You should've done better on the beam! You need to practice that beam! You're heavy and sluggish out there. If I didn't know better, I'd think you were your mother."

Tanya Luckert, a friend of Jennifer's from high school:
I never saw much of Jen's dad. I always thought he was odd, but it didn't really concern me. I do remember that he had a strange laugh. Jen's folks came to our house for a Christmas party one year and Barbara looked like she had been crying a lot—her eyes were red and puffy. She said everything was okay when we asked what had happened. I believe she had a bruise, but I'm not 100 percent sure. I've also seen Barbara in a similar condition on a trip to Lake George. I didn't actually see anything happen, but it seemed like something may have. At the time, I was young and didn't really think about it too much.

Jen was often unhappy. I always knew her parents fought—I could hear them screaming in the background when we were on the phone, but I don't remember thinking that this was why she was sad. I do know that she was unhappy because her parents were fighting in Lake George. She came into our room crying and told us her parents were fighting and she needed to get out of there. We felt terrible, but didn't know the extent of the fight. Parents fight all the time, but we didn't know what was really going on.

The day her dad died, I had just returned to Florida from New York. I was literally stepping out of the car on my way from the airport when my mom called. At that point, no one really knew what had happened, but she told me that Barbara was a suspect in Ray's death. I was completely shocked and felt terrible. Mom said she couldn't stop thinking about how Barbara had been taken away without any shoes on.

I texted Jen because I didn't want to force her to speak to me if she wasn't ready. Why didn't I know what was going on in my best friend's home? I felt terrible that I had not been a better friend and figured it out; I felt terrible for the situation she was going to be in with her father gone and her mom in jail; I felt terrible for being helpless. Then I looked for a flight back to New York.

Note: *My mom was still wearing her fuzzy pink bedroom slippers when she was arrested. She wasn't allowed to put her shoes on.*

As I was getting healthier, Mom decided she needed to educate herself about these types of things, and that's when she discovered the power of the Internet. She had more resources than the *Encyclopedia Britannica* at her fingertips, both at home and at work. Not one to infringe on office time for personal pleasure or instruction, she decided to avail herself of the computer that had once provided such a truce between her and my father.

When she logged on to the AOL account she had named but rarely used, her earlier suspicions of my father's "extracurricular activities"—that he'd taken them outside of their bedroom—were confirmed as Mom was introduced to Instant Messaging in full, graphic glory. There were several messages that kept popping up.

Although she was disturbed and not about to reply to messages clearly unintended for her, she was also curious enough to read the trail of correspondence contained within the instant-message windows. She was sorry she did. He had apparently joined a chat room for people who had . . . similar interests . . . and was engaging in private instant-message conversations with some of the members.

Mom said she felt sick, and thought, *Who are these people? What kind of diseases might Ray be contracting?* She wasn't concerned about catching anything herself; it had been well over a decade since that could have been possible. But Raymond and I sometimes did our homework on the computer and she was terrified that we would see that our father was into something called infantilism—that he preferred other men to dress up like a mommy and whip him while he sexually gratified himself; or that he was willing to switch roles and play the mommy to the other "bad boys" who deserved to be punished in the group.

She had thought his "uniform" and whip and fondness for diapers was disgusting and abnormal, but what he'd forced her to watch and do was mild in comparison to this.

Mom said she could not let us be even remotely exposed to this sickness. She felt a renewed urgency to get out of the house and away from my father, and she needed to do it before he reverted to his old ways of using violence and fatal threats to hold them all hostage.

The last time she had tried to leave, he beat her bloody with the phone. These days, the phones were smaller and more portable, not the kind of weapon that could do much damage. But he had his hands, and although he had not raised them to her for a blessed while, she could not count on it. He also had his guns, which he had not threatened her with recently either, but if he felt threatened, that might change too. And what might he most fear? He had gone to such great lengths to integrate his lifestyle anonymously through the Internet, it reinforced her belief that his real fear was that she would *out* him.

She wondered if that could be our out. Could she use his fear against him and bargain with that—her silence in exchange for our freedom? This would be a delicate high-wire act with everything to gain, everything to lose, and there was a risk he would respond badly. But there was also the possibility he would let us go so he could indulge his perversions to his heart's content and not have to keep up appearances at home. In that regard, it could also be an exchange of *his* freedom for our freedom.

That's how she decided she would put it to him—not like a threat, which could set him off in the wrong direction. The last time she had met with terrible consequences, but this was a different time, and since 9/11, a different man—but one who was showing signs of regressing, so all the more reason to seize the moment before it was gone.

Although she felt her reasoning was sound, it still took Mom over a week to get up the nerve to confront him. But she was determined and her self-esteem was up for the first time in more than twenty years. She had to act on it before she lost it again.

"Ray, I want a divorce. I'm leaving today and I'm taking the kids with me." The words came out in one long breath. Winded but not wanting to be interrupted, she rushed on, "Your lifestyle is your business, but I don't want the kids anywhere near it. I know what you are doing on the computer and the kind of people you're involved with. Now it's time for you to live your life while you let me live mine. Just let me go without a fight and no one will ever know about this."

Swiftly she moved past him and grabbed one of the suitcases she had packed earlier in the day. He didn't try to stop her and she hurried to tell Raymond and me to get enough things together to live out of a suitcase for a few days. She would come home while he was at work and pack more as needed.

Mom had caught him off guard with a strategy that had apparently worked, since he didn't make a peep while we quickly grabbed a few things and were ready to go in minutes. We knew not to ask questions.

The three of us hurried down the stairs, and then Raymond and I waited by the front door while Mom turned to race back up for the other suitcase she had packed. My father came out of nowhere.

"You threaten me?" His eyes were blank and lifeless. He grabbed Mom by the throat and pushed her against the wall near the landing of the staircase. She said that her eyes felt as if they would pop from their sockets from the pressure. She looked at us as we were screaming at him to stop.

"I am going to kill you," he informed her matter-of-factly. "I told you I would if you ever tried to leave again. Why did you not believe me?"

He squeezed tighter. Her airwaves were being crushed, and we thought she was going to die. Her arms flailed wildly, trying to scratch at his hands. Then it was over, and she gasped for air. As quickly as he had appeared, he disappeared, and she was still alive.

Mom slid to the floor. Raymond took off and that scared Mom more than the possibility of being strangled. Raymond's athletic ability had given him a sense of physical power that she feared would be turned on our father. Raymond had a bright future ahead, and she couldn't bear to think of it marred by his being charged with some kind of domestic violence. Such an irony was not out of reason—our father would not hesitate to report him in retaliation. Then there were the psychological scars that he might have to carry, because Raymond is nothing like our father. Thank God! He has a gentle nature.

"Jennifer, go find your brother." Mom wheezed out the words and sucked in another breath of air. "Tell him I need him here with me."

I was able to find him and we did as Mom asked and helped her up, found the cell phone in her purse, and stood by as she began to punch in 9-1-1. Raymond and I were too terrified even to try to make the call.

"Hang up."

Before she could obey or refuse, my father slapped the phone out of her unsteady hands and loomed over her. He turned to us. We were standing close enough to jump him if that's what it took to rescue Mom.

"Don't even think about it," he snarled. "I can call the police, but you can't. I *am* the police. Any cop you call, I'll have them eating out of the palm of my hand. Now back off."

We looked at Mom and she nodded. "Tell them to go upstairs and take their suitcases with them, Barb." When she simply nodded in their direction, he snapped, "Tell them!"

"Raymond. Jennifer. Do as the man says." She told me that she would not say "your father." A real father would never subject his children to a nightmare like this.

"You know the code, Barb. If you or the kids have the cops

come here, they'll look the other way once I tell them I'm one of them. Or maybe you want to try to run off to a shelter? I know where all of them are. I'll find you. You want to take me to court for a divorce, crying that I hurt you? No judge would take your word over—"

"But I don't want to tell them you hurt me, Ray," she interrupted. Her voice was a painful rasp she had to force to be heard. "I don't want to tell anyone anything."

"Shut up, you idiot. I know how to chop you up into little pieces so nobody will be the wiser. I'm not afraid to die, and I will take more than you with me—starting with your daddy. Remember? That's the way it's always been, always will be. First your daddy, then the kiddies, then you, then me. A blaze of glory. That's the only way I'm going out."

Mom realized how grievously she had underestimated his need to keep all of us under his roof and under his thumb. He had too much to lose—his facade. He wasn't vehemently opposed to a divorce because of God or the church. We were the family he had strategically built to mask the true nature of Ray Sheehan. His double life required a charade of normalcy, and Mom, Raymond and I were it.

Mom said she searched through drawers for her purple scarf, but not really seeing. She was in a haze, as when someone looks at her watch to see what time it is but has to look again for it to register. She'd thought about calling in sick. Her throat and neck were bruised with finger marks, and she had a hard time turning her head. Still, she was better off being at work than at home, fearful that my father might make her look at his "trophy" pictures again now that he had reverted to the man who had once terrified her into obedience—and how quickly he had done so again.

Yes, seeing the girls at work would be better for sure, but not without a scarf. Although it certainly wouldn't be the first time she would go to work with marks on her skin. Betsey had seen the evidence along with two other co-workers, Valerie and Eileen, when she had come back from Lake George with two black eyes. He had beaten her unmercifully, once again making her bleed—not to mention the humiliation she suffered in front of friends who were there. He had gotten drunk by the pool and passed out before dinner, so he beat her because she "should've controlled his intake." But mom had yet again convinced herself it was just because he was drunk that he slipped up and that it wouldn't happen again because he'd said so, and otherwise he was behaving so well.

Karen Seara, friend of the family:
Our families were close when our kids were growing up. We first met when Raymond and our son Nick were in preschool. We became closer when the boys played on the same sports teams.

I recall there was talk among the parents about Ray's not playing all the boys on his team, but only a chosen few. I also thought he was tough on the boys.

Ray always carried a gun. He drove entirely too fast and was quick to anger over any difficulties. I remember his pounding on the dashboard and cursing when there was traffic. One night on the way home from dinner, he drove so fast on the Belt Parkway that it terrified us all, and although we begged him to slow down, he refused. We never got in the car with him again.

As for the kids, Raymond always seemed quiet and sullen around his father. Jennifer's severe weight loss became apparent when our families went to Sea Isle City, which is on the Jersey Shore. My husband and I expressed our concerns to both Ray and Barbara at the time. We weren't sure what was going on. We noticed that Raymond and Jennifer often seemed unhappy, but I guess that since we didn't know what was going on, we attributed it to that "growing up" stage that all teens go through.

Through the years, there were several things that I found strange. Barbara always seemed nervous and on edge when we went out. She spent a lot of time texting her children, was often quiet, and didn't participate in the conversation. Anything that went wrong was blamed on Barbara. She was always in a rush and jittery. She wore a lot of cover makeup on her face. She was with Ray at all times and never socialized alone. I never saw Barbara crying, but she seemed sad and unhappy.

I thought it was strange that he seemed to make all the decisions regarding anything—from vacations to household renovations to purchases. He even sold Barbara's car and bought another one without consulting her.

On a skiing trip, Barbara fell out of the family tube; the tube then ran over her, and Ray was more concerned about the camera she was carrying than he was about her.

I often saw bruises on Barbara that she attributed to her "clumsiness," or her "being in the wrong place at the wrong time," or her "rushing," or her "not paying attention."

I remember an incident in particular that left me more than uneasy. We were at Lake George, and Ray had been drinking all afternoon. I went to the Sheehan's room to tell them we were ready for dinner. I heard Ray screaming in their room, and then Barbara and Jen came flying out of the room, closing the door behind them. They looked petrified. Ray was still screaming and cursing inside the room. I asked what was going on. I wanted to go get my husband, but Barbara said no, that

*everything would be fine. She told me just to go on to dinner and they
would follow. But I was uneasy about leaving. She asked me to go—
please go, and assured me that all would be okay. I left, and told my
husband what had happened. We went to dinner, and they followed
about half an hour later.*

*The next morning Barbara came to breakfast wearing sunglasses.
When I asked, "Why the sunglasses?" she lifted them to reveal a black
eye. I asked her what happened and she told me that Jen had said something to Ray and he threw the phone, but it accidentally hit her. I
wasn't convinced and I expressed my concerns to my husband. I asked
him if he thought Ray had hit her. He said if he thought anything like
that was going on he would confront him, but he didn't believe Ray
would do something like that. The memory of that night nagged me for
a long time.*

Mom and Betsey had that connection women often share that
enables them to communicate with no more than a look, and there
was no escaping it when she went into school wearing the purple
scarf around her neck. Betsey's eyes followed her as she walked
toward her desk, and then remained fixed on her, studying her
every move, interpreting her body language. With sporadic
glances and raised eyebrows, Betsey told her, *You know that I know
you need help.* Always discreet, Betsey waited until just before lunch
to confront her.

"Barbara, whatever is happening at home has got to stop. Look
at you. You're a mess." Betsey took one of Mom's shaky hands and
pressed a slip of paper into her palm. She curled her fingers over

the little white strip and whispered, "Call this number. They can help you. You don't have to be alone."

Mom had considered calling a domestic hotline before—she'd even been ready to call 9-1-1 the day before—but this open prompt from a co-worker made her realize how quickly the situation was hurtling back into that dark, dark place. If it got into the open, and Betsey's slip of paper indicated it already had, she had the physical reminder beneath her scarf of how he could react. An outside party's intervention, although her intention was good, might even be the tipping point that would send him over the edge, taking the rest of us with him.

Mom said nothing, but she did fold the paper into a tiny square, and then tucked it into a secret spot in her purse.

CHAPTER ELEVEN

Self-Preservation

"Hunger, love, pain, fear are some of those inner forces which rule the individual's instinct for self-preservation."
—ALBERT EINSTEIN

It was in the summer of 2007 that Raymond wanted to take a trip to Jamaica with his friend Keith and his parents, who graciously invited my parents to go along. Of course, once my father caught wind of this idea, there was no stopping him from accepting the invitation to join them. I was in Spain, studying abroad with my college for the summer semester at the time. Since I didn't go away to college, I really wanted this studying abroad experience. Although my mom was very worried about me, she felt that I deserved this opportunity. I was excited, but at the same time I was apprehensive about leaving my mom and brother behind with my father. I felt that he was spiraling out of control and his behavior was becoming more and more bizarre. He never listened to us about important things going on in our family, or heard any of us when we spoke to him. When my mom told me that they were going to go to Jamaica, part of me thought that would be good because sometimes my vacation father would emerge; but recently he had been acting so strangely that I was worried something terrible was going to happen—I just didn't know what.

Claire Daly, Jennifer's friend from college:
I remember going to Spain with Jennifer Sheehan in the summer of 2007. During this trip, as physically present as Jen was, she was not always mentally or emotionally present. She was often on her cell phone, checking in with her family at home. Jen would typically make sure these phone calls were private, walking away from the group when she made them. Typically, after these phone calls she would make small comments out of frustration, implying she didn't feel that her mom was telling her the truth or giving her detailed information. She would say that she knew her mom was withholding information from her so Jen would fully enjoy her trip, although she was unable to do so anyway, as she often appeared worried. Without knowing the situation, we could tell that Jen had a very strong relationship with her mother and talked about her dad minimally, if at all.

I also noticed that on numerous occasions, Jen would become ill and refrained from participating in trips or other plans. It didn't seem that she was physically ill; however, she appeared extremely nervous and anxious, which caused her to isolate herself. I remember on numerous occasions that those of us who had become close to her during this trip talked regarding our concern for Jen, because we didn't fully know what was going on with her. We girls may not have known at the time what was going on, but we were able to assume it was something serious involving her family—specifically her mom. Looking back on the trip, I remember that Jen became most ill within the last few days prior to leaving. Knowing what I now know, I would assume she became so sick because she was extremely nervous about what she would be going home to.

Weeks before Mr. Sheehan died, Jen sent numerous emails out on

Facebook, and I believe emails to personal email addresses as well. Through these emails, Jen asked everyone to keep their eyes and ears open for any apartment she could rent. Jen stressed in these emails that she needed an apartment immediately and would take anything she/we could find. She didn't explain in much detail about why she wanted to move out—just that she wanted out of her house and that she wanted/needed out as soon as possible.

I was with Jen the day before Mr. Sheehan died. We were getting together with the friends we had made on the Spain trip for a day of girl time. Jen and I planned to meet at my house in the late morning and travel together to meet up with the other girls. However, Jen arrived at my home earlier then we had planned. When I met Jen at the car to tell her that I needed additional time to get ready, she seemed very upset and appeared to have been crying. She apologized for being early, simply saying that she needed to get out of her house. She didn't go into further details as to why, however she was on the phone with her boyfriend, Jesse, and said she'd wait for me while continuing to talk to him.

The drive to meet up with the other girls was long, and during this time Jen told me some more details about her reason for needing out of the house earlier than planned, She said that her parents had gotten into a fight and that her father had hurt her mother and destroyed their home, throwing and breaking items. She also expressed that this was not the first time her father had done something like this and she was confident and fearful that this would not be his last time either.

She said that she had tried to support her mom through this and encouraged her to leave her father, but her mother felt trapped. Jen said that as much as she loved her mother, she could no longer watch her father treat her mother this way, which is why she wanted to move out as soon as possible.

Through the day, we didn't want to push the topic or ask too many questions, so we let Jen say what she was comfortable with, and offered her any support we could. At lunch, she still seemed upset and distant, and had two or three glasses of wine. Although some of the other girls drank as well, Jen is not your typical drinker. For her to have, not one glass of wine, but two or three in the middle of the day was unlike her. It seemed that she was trying to distract herself from her stress and upset state of mind.

Numerous times throughout the day, and in the car on the drive home, Jen was constantly on her cell phone or checking her cell phone. She would say that she was texting with her mom and checking in on how she was. When getting closer to my house so she could pick up her car, Jen appeared extremely upset about returning home. I told her she could stay with me and my family for the night until she felt safe to go home. However, out of fear for her mother's safety and being the loyal daughter that she is, Jen said she needed to go home to be with her mom—but she agreed that if her father acted out again or if she felt unsafe, she would immediately call and stay with me.

The day Mr. Sheehan died, the same girls Jen and I made friends with while in Spain contacted each other via phone to relay the story. One had seen it on the local news, and then I checked the internet. Most of us attended the same school (Molloy College) and decided to meet there to discuss and plan further. Although we all tried to contact Jen on her cell phone, we were unsuccessful. We went to Facebook.com and were able to get Jesse's cell phone number. He was currently stationed out of state, and he confirmed the story. He was at an airport trying to get home to Jen. He said he had spoken to her and she was obviously extremely upset and in shock. Jesse agreed to send Jen our love, well wishes and to keep us updated.

Within a week or so, a few of us met again and called Jen on speakerphone. She told us that when she returned home the night before her dad died, she immediately went to bed, as she had to go to work the next morning. She left the house that morning without seeing any family members because it was so early. When she received the call at work from a neighbor telling her to come home as soon as possible because there was *an emergency, Jen said she expected the worst. She thought her dad had killed her mother and she would be returning home to find that her mother was dead. When she was informed the situation was the other way around, and that her mom had killed her dad in self-defense, she was relieved. The stress she was feeling currently was that her mother was incarcerated for an act of self-defense, and that she wanted her mom to be home with her and her family where she belonged. Jen expressed that she did not want anyone to die as the result of her parents' relationship, but that she supported fully what her mother did, knowing that she had no other choice in the situation. Jen said that although she was upset that her mom was incarcerated, she felt relieved that her mom was now safe because her father was gone.*

Weeks after this phone conversation, we girls were able to meet with Jen for desserts at one of our homes. During our conversations with her, she continued to express that she supported her mother. Jen told us examples of the abuse her mother had suffered, including a situation where her father poured a boiling hot pot of tomato sauce over her mother's head.

Jen also informed us of one of Jesse's first encounters with Mr. Sheehan. They were having dinner in a restaurant—I believe the occasion was Jen's birthday. Mr. Sheehan was very quiet, and then became verbally abusive toward Jen, calling her such names as "whore" or "slut" and informing her that he no longer permitted her to live at home with him. His outburst came out of nowhere and shocked the family and Jesse, as well as extremely embarrassed Jen. She said her father never apologized for this conversation, and typically did not apologize for similar things he would do or say. She used such words as "crazy" or "insane" to describe her father's mental state.

Jen explained that she had barely any contact with her father for years, although they lived in the same house. She was constantly walking on eggshells in her home due to her father's verbal and physical abuse. Jen mentioned that on other occasions, Mr. Sheehan became phys-

ically and verbally aggressive with both her brother and her maternal grandfather, although I do not fully remember the details of these situations. She said Mr. Sheehan did not communicate with her mother's family and tried to stop her mom from communicating with them as well. Jen also discussed that her father tried to have complete control over her mother, checking her receipts after shopping to control the finances, timing her mother when she went to work or out anywhere.

From what Jen described, living with Mr. Sheehan was a constantly stressful, anxiety-provoking and unsafe environment (emotionally, mentally and physically) for her, her mother and her brother. However, since Mr. Sheehan's passing, I believe the household is the complete opposite. As Mrs. Sheehan reported on the Today Show, their house is now a home. Jen and her mom can now communicate happily, without Jen's needing to be worried or anxious to make phone calls to her home.

Jen herself appears a lot happier, and "lighter" if that makes sense. She says she feels as though a huge weight has been lifted off her shoulders, and that she can now live her life without holding herself back out of fear of what her father will do to her mother.

Jen continues to be her mom's biggest supporter and an amazingly strong person that I admire greatly.

It was no secret that my father loved to travel, especially to tropical places, so his response to the Jamaica trip was no surprise. But Mom thought he seemed particularly determined to make this trip and suspected he was also planning on some fetish sex in Jamaica that he had prearranged over the Internet. He would need his cover in order to go, and she was it. She would have to accompany him or risk his wrath. As much as she loathed the idea, she went to Jamaica.

Any hope she might have had that "Vacation Ray" might show up was immediately squelched. She had to wear a cover-up by the second day. If he drank too much, it was her fault. When she asked him if he would be back in time for dinner from one of his solo outings, he slapped her around for that, too. Socializing too much with the other parents resulted in a beating.

One evening, they were supposed to meet the other parents at the hotel bar for a pre-dinner cocktail before heading off to a reserved table. My father had been drinking by the pool all day, so when the time came for them to get ready, he didn't object to Mom's taking a shower first while he rested. When she came out, he was asleep. She tried to wake him, but he was really out of it, so she finished dressing for the evening and went to the appointed cocktail hour to let everyone know they were running a little behind and would meet them in the restaurant. In reality, however, she still had to get him up, and given the marathon showers he was notorious for, she didn't see how they'd make dinner at all.

"I told them you were already in the shower," she explained after waking him up.

"Why did you let me sleep? It's your fault I drank too much."

It was futile to argue with him, to explain that she was not responsible for his actions or for the fact that they were now late for dinner. Figuring that he would be angry with her no matter what, and not wanting to further embarrass my brother, she said, "I'm going on down to dinner and when you're ready you can meet us there."

As she turned to leave the room, he latched on to a fistful of her hair and grabbed the back of her neck like the scruff of a cat. "Don't you be so smug—I'll fix you."

He slammed Mom's forehead against the cinderblock wall adjacent to the door of the room, splitting it open. Blood was flowing freely, but he then raced her across the room to the window and threw her head into the corner next to the air-conditioning unit. More blood. The ragged cracks between the cinderblocks snagged the tip of her nose each time her head met with another wall.

"Stop! No! Please, Ray, no more!"

In response, he banged her head against each corner of the room and laughed. He kicked her, choked her, punched her and stepped on her repeatedly. He almost killed my mom in that Jamaican hotel. When he finally stopped, her face was covered with blood.

"All right then," he said with eerie cheer. "Let's get you cleaned up now so we can go to dinner."

As he used the hotel towels to clean up the laceration on her head, Mom cried and twitched in pain, worrying about what her face looked like and how much damage he had done to her this time. She said that her head was pounding, throbbing with pain. He eventually realized that it was so deep and large that it was going to take numerous stitches, and he had no choice but to take her to the hospital. He refused even to let Mom look in the mirror to see the damage he had just caused to her face.

But before leaving the room, he wagged his finger in her face and once again his eyes were blank and expressionless. He said, "Remember . . . good girls don't tell. And bad girls die if they do."

Mom remained silent in the hotel lobby, pressing a white bath towel against her head. She later told my brother and me that the pain in her head was so bad she thought she would faint, and she was so worried about what a hospital in Jamaica would be like, and how they would stitch her face—while my father calmly finished explaining to the receptionist that, "My wife slipped while getting out of the shower and hit her head on the vanity counter. She cut it open really bad so could you call us an ambulance, please?"

Oh, he was cool under pressure; something he was taught as an NYPD law enforcement officer. I can just see him going into Sergeant Sheehan-mode. Mom said that she wanted to scream, "*My husband just tried to kill me,*" but such an act could put the first nail in her coffin.

My dad actually then walked over to the table in the restaurant where my brother sat with Keith and his parents. Mom didn't say a word as my father told his smooth lie again. Although Keith and his parents were shocked and concerned, Raymond wouldn't even look at him.

One more time, he told his story to the EMT in the ambulance on the way to the hospital, and the technician bought the explanation as quickly as the others had. Mom said she didn't care if the medical facility turned out to be substandard in comparison to those in New York; she was simply grateful not to be alone with my father.

The nurses were attentive, and the doctor was kind, especially while he stitched her up and expressed his concern that she had a concussion. Believing that my father would provide the necessary caretaking during the critical hours after a head injury, the doctor gave him instructions on the signs he should watch for. The medical staff administered antibiotics, a standard tetanus shot, and sent her back to the hotel with her "doting" husband.

Raymond spotted her before she could make it to the room to lie down. Mom said that as he was walking up to her, the look in his eyes said it all. She had seen it many times before—the hurt, the weariness, the rage. "What happened?"

"Oh you know me, I'm such a klutz. I fell in the shower." But my brother knew—he also knew how the Sheehan Family Lie worked.

Raymond reached his arm around her, locking Mom into the safety he could provide as long as he didn't leave her side and the coward who beat her didn't have a gun. He despised our father, as did I, and Mom knew that we did. She told me that it made her sad that our father was a man who made a mockery of what it meant to be a husband and father. Raymond had somehow emerged from our damaged upbringing with all the positive attributes of manhood that our father lacked.

When my mom was back in the hotel room and was finally able to look at herself in the mirror, she couldn't see how far the stitches spanned because they jumped the hairline, but when she gingerly explored the damage, they seemed to end at the crown of her head.

Debbie, Ronald and Keith Ferrara, friends of the family:
Raymond went to high school at St. Francis Prep with our son, Keith. We socialized a lot as families, especially after football games and at other high school functions. We first met Ray at a football game, and we thought he was a decent family man.

Some of the other parents felt that he was too hard on Raymond during football games. He was very loud and boisterous, and yelled out at the field a lot, but most of the time he tried to be life of the party by speaking loudly. They also thought he was sometimes rude and disrespectful to Barbara. We noticed that he blamed everything that happened on her.

I saw bruises on Barbara once in a while, but the major thing we remember was a trip to the island of Jamaica, which took place in July of 2007, when Barbara received head stitches and bruises on her face and body. The only time we saw Barbara crying was after that incident.

We were waiting for Barbara and Ray to meet the three of us and Raymond for dinner. Barbara came down to say that Ray was running late. She was dressed and had her makeup on, ready for dinner, but appeared a bit nervous. She said we should go to the restaurant and she was going to go back upstairs to hurry Ray up so they would meet us at dinner. A little while later, Barbara and Ray came into the restaurant and Barbara had a bloody towel held tightly to her head. The three of us jumped up to say, "What happened?" Barbara remained very quiet and said nothing but Ray said that she fell in the bathroom getting out of the shower and hit her head on the sink. He said an ambulance was on the way and that they would be going to the hospital.

We felt that the strangest part of the incident is that Raymond never raised his head or asked his mom what happened. He put his head down on the table and just shook it. Raymond and his mom are very close and we felt this was a strange way for him to react. We realized afterward that he must have known in his heart that his father did this to his mom. We also couldn't figure out how Barbara had fallen getting out of the shower when she was dressed and had makeup on about a half hour earlier.

The day after this happened, Ray blamed himself for what happened. He told Ronald that it was all his fault and that he felt really bad about it. We didn't understand why he was blaming himself at the time, but realize now why. Barbara had a big bandage on her head after the incident and wore a cover-up the rest of the vacation.

We always thought Raymond was very quiet. He spent a lot of time at our house, especially during his high school years, since he and Keith were best friends. But he hardly said hello to anyone, even though he was very well mannered and respectful. We believe now that he was unhappy about his home life. Now Raymond is completely different— he is still reserved and respectful, but he has a lot more fun and is much friendlier.

The Sheehan Family Lie was precarious, but Mom somehow held it together long enough to get both of us more or less out on our own. I was about to graduate from college, and Raymond had just entered Sacred Heart University in Connecticut. For his talent and hard work in high school sports, he was awarded a college football scholarship. As I have mentioned, I didn't go away to college; I couldn't have dealt with the anxiety of wondering what my father might do if Mom were left alone in the house with him.

While most young men and their families would be thrilled about a sport scholarship, Raymond was hesitant to accept his well-deserved reward since it would take him too far away to keep a perpetual eye on Mom's safekeeping. Mom and I convinced him that I would let him know if we needed his help.

Neither of us at this point was aware of what Mom had kept from us regarding our father's sex life, and how he had forced her to listen to his accounts of being with other partners and made her watch things on the computer. She was relieved that Raymond and I had our own laptops by this time and had no interest in their computer.

When Raymond left for college, Mom missed him terribly. She said that she cried day and night for a week, yet she felt it was the right thing for him to do—and it was only a three-hour round trip; just the right distance to get him away from our father and into a good university. This was definitely doable for Mom. She devised a routine that would get her out of the house on weekends, while remaining an active and integral part of Raymond's life. She would pick up and drop off his laundry, and thanks to the Internet, proofread the papers he e-mailed for her review. Unlike the typical college freshman, he texted her several times a day, checking in to make sure she was "okay" and "not hurt." Mom wanted him to enjoy college and spend his energy on sports, studying, and girls, instead of worrying about her.

The best way she knew to make that happen was to convince him that she was fine and that his father was acting more like his "Vacation Ray" self. This was her goal when she and my father started out on their late-morning drive to watch one of Raymond's first college football games—this one an away game at the University of Albany. They left as planned around eleven in the morning and arrived at two that afternoon, which put them there plenty ahead of start-time, and they beat a good portion of the traffic.

When they arrived on campus, my father dropped Mom off in front of the stadium and said he was going to look for somewhere to park the car. She didn't see him again for three hours.

He had the tickets and left her stranded in the parking lot. His phone went straight to voicemail each time she called him over the three-hour period. She wasn't about to call Raymond, who was exactly where he should be—with his team doing warm-ups for the game that, eventually, she could hear in full swing while she sat on the curb.

He finally showed up, sauntering her way with a grin on his face.

By then Mom was too upset to be afraid. Besides, there were enough ticket-takers and hawkers still around to keep her relatively safe from a backlash. "Where were you? Why did you leave me? Why did you turn off your phone?"

"Stop your whining. Let's go watch the game. If they play him, hopefully he won't fuck anything up and be an embarrassment to the family."

They didn't speak for the entire game; or at least what was left of it. Amid the yells of the cheerleaders, the sounds of the marching band, and the cheering fans, Mom mentally rehearsed being normal for Raymond after the game. The last thing she wanted was to cause him to leave this safe place and return to our special little piece of hell. Given his big hug and happy wave good-bye as she and my father left, she had pulled it off.

The next day it became clear where my father had been for the three hours he was missing. When she logged on to the home computer to check her e-mails, the chat room IMs popped up, confirming what he had been doing during that time.

It was December of 2007 and Raymond's eighteenth birthday. He had been at college for a whole semester and everyone was excited to have him home for the holiday break, so this family gathering was special. Poppop and Uncle Michael were in the living room with my father and his brother Vincent, along with Robin's second husband, Mike, who gave Raymond a high five and asked for his autograph.

The women were all in the kitchen, laughing and gossiping

and trading ideas about recipes while seeing to dinner preparations. Mom was in her element, loving every second of this opportunity to bond with the other women while the men sat around the television watching football and noshing on chips and dips, and the beer she served to wash it all down.

Just before halftime, my father's voice bellowed over the noise from the Jet's game and the clanking of dishes in the kitchen. While Mom and Linda made several trips to transport hot casserole dishes from the kitchen to the dining room, the noise level turned from loud to ugly. There were enough snippets caught along the way to realize that what had started off as a benign sports debate had turned into a heated argument spinning out of control.

More specifically, my father was spinning out of control. Something during this conversation set him off, or maybe it was the beer that allowed the monster to emerge—not all the way out, but enough to turn his face and neck an eggplant color while he called the other men "shits," "dumbasses," and "stupid fucks," with most of the obscenities directed at my grandfather.

Poppop is not a confrontational man. As my father hit his boiling point, my grandfather stood up and began to walk out, intent on removing himself from the situation. Before he could do so, my father got into his face and shouted, "Get out of my house, you fucking cock! And never come back!"

Nanni looked like a little pit bull as she charged toward my father, stopping short at his feet. Uncle Michael had tried to grab her, but she was too quick. She shook her finger in his face and shouted back, "You're a real piece of shit. You were always a piece of shit, and you are still . . . a piece of shit."

With those last words, they immediately left the house, along with Uncle Michael and his family, and Aunt Robin and Uncle Mike. Raymond and I had all we could take, so we left too, to drive around and talk. After informing Mom that she was never to have contact with any of them ever again, he slammed out of the house as well. Of course, unfortunately, he wouldn't stay gone for long.

Mom sat in the kitchen and sobbed while Linda and Vincent tried to comfort her. Then something broke inside of her. In so many ways, Mom's family was all she had outside of our hell, and their Sundays together were sacred to her. My father had profaned that. He had ripped apart the fragile fabric that was holding her life together. After all the beatings and perversions and abuses he had so generously dished out through the years, this is what sent her to a point of critical mass.

My mom realized at this point that she could no longer protect the secret she had been keeping for years. My father had finally crossed a line—the line of no return. In one way it was a relief for her, because now she could finally tell the story and not be the one that opened the can of worms; he did it himself by exploding in front of so many people. She finally believed that she would be able to leave this monster.

She sat at her kitchen table and poured out the horror of her twenty-four-year marriage. She was surprised at how unsurprised Linda and Vincent were, and they even offered their help. They said they should have known—all the warning signs were there and they failed to pick up on them. They told my mom they were sorry for not being there to help her and promised to be there from that moment on.

Raymond's Memories

On any holiday that focused on my mom, like her birthday or Mother's Day, things were worse because it was her day. He didn't want her to have any positive attention. He would find something to flip out over; if she had placed a picture to the left on a table, he would scream at her because it should be on the right.

But there were family get-togethers on other holidays and birthdays, and he was careful not to let others see what he was like—he would just give Mom threatening looks to keep her in line. We noticed them, but others didn't. Mom, Jen and I looked forward to these occasions because it was the only time when we felt relatively safe. Yet even at those times, we could never let our guard down—we never knew what might set him off. And on my eighteenth birthday something did, and he verbally attacked my grandfather— my mom's dad. This was the first time he had done any-thing like this in front of others, and I realized that he had lost control and didn't care anymore. It was a turning point. My mom's parents and the rest of her family left. Jen and I left the house to take a drive and talk about what had hap-pened, and how we couldn't deal with it anymore. Eventu-ally, Jen's cell phone rang and it was Dad. He told her that we had better get back home to protect our mother's life or something bad was going to happen.

Michael and Allison Henry, Barbara's brother and sister-in-law:
I don't remember Ray and Barbara's first date. I am seven years younger than Barbara, so of course Allison and I were not dating yet and I was

still in elementary school at the time. I liked most of the guys that Barbara dated before Ray and most of them were nice to me.

At first, I thought Ray was a nice guy, I guess I hoped that he could be like a big brother to me. However, after they got engaged, although he still seemed nice to me, things began to change. I started to think he was a little weird from the way he treated my sister and how she stopped going out as much with her friends like she used to. Barbara always liked to have a great time, laughing, dancing and just having fun, but her personality started changing at this point. I was still young so I was not too concerned, but I do remember thinking it was strange.

Allison and I began dating the year Jennifer was born. We were young ourselves, but I was so proud to be an uncle. We adored Jennifer, but it seemed that Ray didn't want us to watch her—like he had some kind of problem when we were with her.

After Raymond was born in 1989, Allison and I were both happy to be part of his life as well. But this was the point that we started noticing a real change in Ray. We felt that he began to become withdrawn at family functions and many times we were uncomfortable in his presence.

We noticed that he blamed everything on my sister, Barbara. No matter what it was, it was her fault. We recall many instances about Ray's unpredictable and abusive behavior. One of the major incidents that come to mind is my bachelor party in August of 1997. We were at a local bar, and Ray got so drunk that he couldn't stand up. He wound up giving his loaded gun to one of my uncles (who was not a police officer) and allowed my uncle to hold on to it. He then had a fight with a friend and broke bottles. He was totally out of control and acting irrational. We all had a lot to drink, but I remember worrying about what he was going to do when he got home and hoped that he didn't take out the fact that he drank too much with the guys on my sister.

Ray would put everyone else down by trying to build himself up. If

Allison and I bought a new car, he went out and bought one. He always had to have one thing better than the next person.

As the years went on this became more and more noticeable. He was treating my sister and her children with so little respect. He would put Barbara down in front of everyone—make fun of her and try to make her look stupid. We would notice bruises or black eyes and she always had an excuse. I could not even fathom how a man could put a hand on a woman, so at this point the furthest thing from my mind was that he was hurting her physically.

Allison and I would discuss this, but I felt that if Barbara needed me she knew she could count on me 24/7—I am her brother. So we tried not to get involved. He started to arrive extremely late for every function we had and my sister would sometimes look distant and was no longer acting like the sister I had known for all these years. She was always nervous, stuttering, jittery and just not herself. Whether he was there or not, Barbara was always worried, always jumpy.

He thought he was better than everyone else. He thought he knew everything and his opinion was always right whether it be sports, cars or jobs. His speech was very disrespectful, and at times downright cruel to everyone, but especially to Barbara, Jennifer and Raymond. As time went on, he became more outspoken and was extremely confrontational.

It depended on the day if we felt comfortable around him or if we even liked him. Sometimes he would be okay and we could have a beer and some laughs. But those times were far and few between. And as the years went on they became non-existent. We always felt we had to be careful of what we said around him.

Another thing we noticed is that Jennifer and Raymond were not close to their father. He never showed them any kind of compassion, affection or love. They were very close to my sister and always hugged her and kissed her, but never him.

There were many instances that we can recall feeling uncomfortable around Ray, but the worst one came in December 2007. At this point, it became more apparent how badly he was treating his family. We wanted to interfere, but just felt that maybe it appeared worse than it was.

It was Raymond's 18th birthday in December and we were all at my sister's house, including Ray's brother and sister-in-law. The men were watching TV in the living room when a discussion came up about sports. One thing lead to another and Ray called my father a dick or a cock—something along those lines. I lost it. All the tension from watching him treat my sister and niece and nephew so horribly for all these years had built up and words were exchanged. Allison and I decided to take our children and go home. We did not want them subjected to this horrible scene. Looking back, I wish I hadn't left my sister and her children with this disgusting man, but at the time I needed to protect my family also. He was completely out of control.

We were in Florida at my mom and dad's condo when we found out what happened on February 18, 2008. I don't remember the exact feelings, but I know we were shocked—but also relieved that he had not hurt my sister or her children. We packed up our family and immediately went back to New York.

We feel regret that we didn't know how bad the situation was. We should have been able to help Barbara, Jennifer and Raymond. Ray's brother and sister-in-law knew the extent of the problems and it is unimaginable how they did nothing to help my sister, her children or even their own brother. Vincent was very close to our family. My Aunt Marie told us that he came to the scene that day and asked her, "Who was it, Aunt Marie?" She answered, "It was Ray." He then said, "I thought it would have been the other way around."

I am not sure how they can live with themselves knowing all the heartache and pain they have caused by not stepping in.

We are both so proud of how well Jennifer and Raymond have turned out, and we are also proud of my sister. She defended herself and her family.

Note: *I remember my mom telling me a story about my Uncle Michael's bachelor party that took place in August 1997, so I was about 11 years old at the time. She told me that the beating my father gave her that night was one of the worst in their marriage. My brother and I were not awake when he came home that night and as our mom did so many times throughout her marriage, she closed our bedroom doors and prayed that we would not see how drunk our father was. My mom described that night as horrifying and brutal. He came home from the party so drunk that he could hardly walk. When my mom went down the stairs to try to help him get up to bed, my father went berserk. He blamed her because he had given someone his loaded gun in the bar and couldn't remember who it was or what they did with it. He began hitting her and then kept beating her with his shoe and his fists. He threw her down and stomped on her ankle and leg with such force that she later was diagnosed with a partially torn Achilles' tendon. As a nurse, I know how strong the Achilles' tendon is, so you can just imagine the brute force he used on her that night. He also beat her on the side of her face with his shoe while he spit in her eyes. The vicious beating to the side of her head resulted in a broken eardrum, diagnosed the next day when she went to the doctor.*

Mike Catanzarite, Barbara's brother-in-law:
My first impression of Ray Sheehan was that he was a loud-mouthed phony with a loud, annoying laugh. There wasn't anything about him that I liked. When he drank, he got nasty. Ray always wanted to be noticed—he was a showoff.

I never met Ray's dad, but his mother appeared to be a tough woman, and she was never happy. I thought both of his brothers were strange. The twin brother, Vincent, had a nervous twitch and the priest, Dan, impressed me as being a phony.

Barbara was always in a rush and nervous. At the end, I could see that she had noticeable bruises. The kids were withdrawn—especially Raymond. Jennifer seemed to have some health issues.

I sometimes question God. Why would this bad thing happen to such a good person—to Barbara—and our family?

The day it happened was unbelievable—unexpected. It was the worst day in all of our lives. It took a toll on the whole family and everyone close to them. This day will never be forgotten. The family stayed united and wanted to help Barbara and the kids in any way they could. There has been nothing but support from friends and family. This was self-defense, not murder.

It was a tragedy, but it could have been worse—it could have been the other way around.

The next morning, Linda followed through on her offer to help. She called Mom's office and left her a message containing the number of a domestic violence hotline.

Mom knew that she had to take action. That had become clear to her on the Jamaica trip, and it was confirmed the day of Raymond's Birthday. My father was no longer careful about hiding his abuse. Even though he had given her a short reprieve after they returned home from Jamaica, she thought it was probably due to the severity of the beating combined with the fact there were outside witnesses.

He had gone to a place in his abuse that night where he hadn't gone before—his abuse was now public. His blowup on Raymond's birthday was another frightening indication that things were about to come to a head. Mom's intuition and survival instinct told her that she was soon destined for a beating that would put her in a body bag. She knew he wanted her dead because he told her so. "The next time I get you alone, you better watch out, bitch."

My mom explained to Raymond and me that although it's hard to understand, after someone has been abused for so many years [as she had been] you know when the end is near. You know when the abuser [our father] loses all regard for his life and the life of his family. He becomes outwardly abusive and his eyes show no emotion at all—they are just blank. Our father was at this point.

She desperately did not want to be alone with him, but he had forbidden my grandparents and everyone else in Mom's family to come over, and she didn't dare pull them into her orbit of danger. Vincent and Linda weren't banned from the house, but she loved them and so kept her distance. That left Raymond and me. The three of us had been in this poisonous stew for as long as we could remember.

When I was about eight or ten, I remember walking down the block with my friend Christie when she said, "My parents were fighting and I was almost afraid he was going to hit her."

I said, "Your father doesn't hit your mother?" Christie was shocked at such a question and said "No!" I just said, "Oh." But for me, there was a lot more to it—this changed everything.

We never talked to our friends about what went on in our house. I was afraid he would kill her, and I didn't think people would take it seriously. I also worried about who they would tell and it might get back to him. We learned to have friends over only if he wasn't there. One time I had a friend sleep over, and we woke up to Dad cursing and screaming at Mom, throwing things because he overslept and it was her fault.

As much as she didn't want us to feel responsible for her, Mom said she was grateful that I was living at home and Raymond visited from college more frequently. His proximity was like a bulletproof vest that Mom wanted to hide behind, but for his own sake, she didn't want him to spend too much time at home, away from the safety of his campus.

Raymond's Memories

When Jen and I were young kids, we thought all families were like ours—that all kids' fathers got into bad moods and abused their mothers. I was in the sixth or seventh grade when I saw that other kids' parents had a good relationship and that they would talk. That's when I realized that my family wasn't normal.

We didn't say anything to Dad about the way he treated Mom, because it would be worse for her. When Jen was younger, she would tell him to stop and say, "Why are you doing this? This is wrong." But he would hit Mom more and scream more. Then she stopped saying anything. When I was about six or seven I wanted to tell Nanni and Pop, my mom's parents, what was going on, but Mom said it would make things worse—and I knew even then that it would. He would often say when he was in a rage, "I will kill you all." We believed that if we told anyone what was going on, he would kill us. He always had his gun next to him. When he was eating, he would take it out of the ankle holster and place it on the table. He also had a gun he wore at his waist. While watching television, it would be next to him on the couch. Even when he was no longer a cop he carried it around—like when we went out to dinner.

There was no tenderness between our parents. Neither of us remembers Dad ever saying anything nice to Mom, nor can we think of even one happy family memory. There were times that things were okay, but there was always tension.

During Mom's trial, the prosecution had me on the witness stand for four hours one day and three hours the next, grilling me about why I left home if I was so worried about my mom; why didn't I take pictures of her bruises; why didn't I go to the police.

There were times when I thought maybe I should kill him and get it over with, but I mostly considered killing myself. All through high school I thought about suicide. I felt frustrated and helpless. There was nothing I could do to help Mom; there was no way out. I thought it was the only way I could escape from him. His guns were always around and I went as far as picking the gun up and holding it. It's the reason I chose to go away to college. I had received a scholarship, and I knew I couldn't live with him any longer. The thoughts of suicide stopped when I got away from him.

Jennifer was in Spain learning Spanish, and I was in Jamaica with a friend and his parents and my parents, when my dad so severely injured my mom that she had to be taken to the hospital in an ambulance—and after that bout of violence, he flipped a switch, lied smoothly that she had fallen in the shower, and got about the business of enjoying his vacation. He could do the most hideous things to her and then laugh.

I asked Mom after my eighteenth birthday incident why she didn't divorce him. Her answer didn't surprise me or Jen—we knew the answer. How could she divorce him? He was a detective with the NYPD. He would find her, kill her, and then make her disappear. She knew that he would kill her—and us too.

Mom had the hotline numbers that both Linda and Betsey had given her. She retrieved the paper she had folded into a tiny square out of a hidden compartment in her purse and looked at the two phone numbers. With her decision made, she placed the call from her car, innocently parked at work. Her feelings were mixed as she punched in the number—a mixture of anxiety, anticipation and fear of the unknown. She wasn't quite sure what she would say or how they'd respond, but she knew that after this call, her life would never be the same.

When the person who answered identified himself as Patrick, she was surprised by the male voice. Her first impulse was to hang up. But just as quickly, she reasoned that speaking to a man about being beat up by a man couldn't possibly be more awkward than seeing a male gynecologist, and the one who had delivered Raymond and me had done a perfectly fine job, so perhaps this Patrick would be good at his—and he was.

Patrick was patient, kind, and empathetic. He didn't make Mom feel that he was judging her. He completely understood why she had stayed in the marriage for so long and why she was still afraid to leave, even though she had every reason to believe her death was only a matter of time—and that time could be imminent if something pushed my father over the thin line he seemed to be straddling.

She could have been on the phone for days if she'd tried to tell him of all the bruises, beatings, and threats of over twenty years, so she gave Patrick a shortened version that ended with, "He's now forbidden me to see my family. He says he'll kill my father, my children, me, and then himself if I try to leave. He is a retired police officer and says he will know if I call the cops and that if I try to hide in a shelter, he will be able to find me. I know he can do everything he says, and once he has nothing to lose, he will."

"You are in the most dangerous of situations," Patrick responded. Mom told me that he had the uncanny ability to keep his voice calm and steady, while still communicating a sense of urgency. He told her that if my father had deluded himself into believing his association with the NYPD made him above the law, then she couldn't just leave. She needed to disappear and make sure her children were in a safe place when she did. He further informed her that this could not be a temporary or local escape. She would have to make herself invisible and disappear indefinitely, because she was correct in believing her husband would not only find her, there was the likelihood that he would also hurt outsiders who might be protecting her. She needed to devise a plan that included the following points:

1. Stash money away to live on when you leave.

2. Have a copy of the car key made so you have access to the car when he takes your car keys away each night.

3. Choose a hiding spot in the house in case he attacks.

4. Be sure to have all your important papers with you when you leave, such as birth certificate, passport, social security card, etc., because once you are gone, there will be no chance of going back.

5. Find a trusted individual to be your emergency contact.

6. Keep your cell phone on you at all times, even when you sleep.

Upon ending the phone call, Mom wasted no time in following Patrick's directions. She even spoke to the assistant principal at her school and then asked Betsey to be her emergency contact. My father wasn't aware of Betsey's existence, but Betsey had become well acquainted with his volatile and irrational behavior, thanks to the incessant phone threats he'd been making since nearly strangling Mom the last time she tried to leave. He shamelessly made calls to the school office, only now he did it daily—more like hourly—and wasn't afraid to yell at anyone else who answered the phone. There was no doubt in Mom's mind that my father was *losing it,* so she knew Patrick was right. When she left, she would have to vanish or risk the safety of any good Samaritans willing to help her out. She wasn't sure if he would go after his own brother and sister-in-law who had certainly been kind to her over the years. Linda had even provided the number to the domestic hotline that had been such a godsend. It was a moot point because she would never put them in a position to be in his line of fire. However, if there was any sense of reason left in his demented mind, she felt he would adhere to that one family value ingrained in the Sheehans—blood is thicker than water. It might possibly be the only value she and my father had in common.

I was practically out of college by this time and could at least financially fend for myself. Once Mom was out of the house, she felt that I would finally feel free to live life on my own terms, and get my own place. She thought we could try to remove ourselves from my father's immediate vicinity at the same time, but she didn't know if that was feasible or, most important to her, if it would give me enough protection once she made her escape.

Mom said that even thinking about the word *escape* made her feel sick. This was the only life she knew. Her family was the be-all and end-all of her world. Was she truly willing to leave everyone and everything behind? Becoming a ghost was in many ways the worst fate she could possibly imagine. What a terrible trade-off, to leave her roots, her family, Raymond and me, and her job in order to stay alive. It was like being asked if she would rather be lethally injected or stoned to death.

She made herself focus on one thing at a time, and first, she had to get away. Her best chance for doing that was by implementing the strategy Patrick had strongly encouraged her to stay focused on. The last thing he tried to impress upon her was the supreme importance of avoiding situations and behaviors that might act as triggers to my father's abuse. She needed to stay on alert for any signs of impending outbursts and not send up any red flags that would put him on alert. *Don't set him off* became her mantra. The ultimate goal was to stay relatively unharmed for as long as it took to get enough cash together and mentally prepare herself for an indefinite goodbye to her old life.

In order to survive, Mom knew that she must leave him before it was too late; she knew that she would not survive the trip to Florida he had booked for February 18, 2008.

"My life depends on canceling this trip," Mom explained in hushed tones to Raymond and me in our kitchen. "His plan is to kill me in Florida, bury me there, and come back alone with some cockamamie story about how I left him." This was his latest threat, and Mom had no reason to believe he was lying.

The problem, as always, was how to get out of his reach long enough to get away. Mom was still mulling over this dilemma the day before the scheduled Florida trip. The morning of February 17, they were in the car and heading up to see Raymond at school. Mom didn't want my father to make this trip up to Connecticut with her. She wanted to go alone and spend this short amount of time with Raymond—just the two of them. This was so important to her, because she knew it might be the last time she saw Raymond for however long, she just didn't know. But my father wouldn't hear of it. He insisted on going with her.

My brother and I did not want her to go on the Florida trip alone with our father. We were terrified of him and we were very aware of how dangerous he had become. He wanted our mother dead.

Mom had told my father the night before that she was not going to Florida with him, and she had told him for the two or three weeks leading up to February 18 that she wasn't going with him. He had ignored her. During the car ride to Connecticut, with more conviction this time, she said, "I'm not going to Florida tomorrow with you, Ray. You'll have to go without me."

"You're going. I took off from work for the week, and there's no way in hell you are embarrassing me by canceling."

"I'm not going to Florida," she reiterated, hating the tremor in her voice. "I'm afraid that what happened in Jamaica will happen again. I don't want to be alone with you in Florida, Ray. I'm afraid."

"Yeah, right. Whatever." He pulled to an abrupt stop by the side of the road and confiscated her keys and wallet. "You're going whether you like it or not."

He peeled back onto the asphalt and pinched her so hard that her skin broke. His reach was long, and the pinch was merely the prelude to an unending sequence of pokes, slaps, and shoves. When they reached the toll of the Whitestone Bridge, Mom imagined performing a stop, drop, and roll, but a yank to her earlobe brought her closer to the driver's seat than out the passenger door.

Traffic added fuel to the fire, and with each "shmuck" or "asshole" who didn't know how to drive in his lane, he described, step-by-step, how he would kill her and then hide her body. Mom explained to Raymond and me that she was more terrified of him at this point than ever before. She said she kept having flashbacks of the crime scene photos he examined so carefully, over and over again.

She hurt all over by the time they arrived at Raymond's dorm. Not that anyone could tell. My father was sufficiently self-protective that he reverted to making sure the bodily harm wasn't easily visible, and Mom was ferociously protective of Raymond, not wanting him to suffer any consequences of embarrassment or questions about his parents. She made sure her clothes and hair covered any visible evidence of my father's inflictions.

They met Raymond at the dorm with smiles on both their faces. When my brother could get Mom aside, she assured him that he shouldn't worry, all was well for the moment, and she relished that moment with Raymond until it was time to leave.

When she kissed Raymond goodbye, she did so in the literal sense and pressed her cheek against his warm, young chest. Mom said that tears welled up in her eyes as she thought this might be the last time she would see Raymond for a very long time; or maybe never see him again.

Mom could feel the dread the minute she shut the door to the car. Before they even left the parking lot on the campus, he jabbed the left side of her nose. Of course, there were no other cars around or pedestrians to witness it. He knew better than that.

"Now, where were we?" His voice was like syrup. "Oh, yeah, you're going to Florida. And by the way, if you get blood on my new car I'll kill you before we get there."

Bleeding heavily from her nose, Mom frantically searched for something to stop the flow. With nothing more than her clothes to stanch it, she undid the seat belt and managed to get out of the blouse she was wearing. She used it as a compress while he sped down the Merritt Parkway—one of the oldest parkways in the United States. Tour books tout it as a scenic route to relish—but for Mom, it was a dark and dangerous stretch of deserted highway, winding through a swath of forest. She prayed that the bleeding would somehow stop because her shirt had quickly absorbed all it could and it was starting to drip onto the leather seats of his car. She told us how much pain she was in and how frightened she was. She couldn't bear to look at herself in the mirror and see the damage he had done to her face this time.

Sitting in the seat wearing just a bra, clasping the blood-soaked shirt to her nose, Mom hadn't thought to put her seatbelt back on. He must have noticed and decided to take advantage of the opportunity. They were driving through the middle of the woods by that time. He slowed down, reached across her, opened her passenger door, and tried to shove her out—but she held on to the door for dear life.

He cursed her, screamed at her, and threatened to kill her all the way home that night, especially since his attempt to push her out of the car had failed.

When they got home my father went inside, taking her keys and wallet with him, leaving Mom on her own to follow. She wondered if it were possible for a person to acquire a tolerance for physical abuse. She could still walk when most people would have passed out from the pain of the bodily damage and the shock.

I wasn't at home when they got back. Mom had warned me to stay away; she knew the refusal to go to Florida would meet with an inevitable backlash. She now knew that the backlash could very well be fatal.

She made it to the bathroom, cleaned herself up as best she could and put on some clothes. The hospital was too far away to walk in her condition, not to mention that it was the middle of February in a very cold part of the country, but she had to get out of the house, as far away from him as possible, even if it was just the front yard. That's where she was when she was so out of options that she called Linda for help. She explained what he had done to her nose and how terrified she was that he was going to kill her that night. Linda was very frightened for her, and told Mom that she agreed with her—that she couldn't go to Florida alone with my father. All of a sudden, out of nowhere he sneaked up behind her and seized the cell phone he had forgotten to confiscate.

"You wanna go to the hospital? I'm coming with you. Get in the car."

He guided her head into the car. Then, pointing to a box of bullets and a gun he had placed near her feet, he threatened, "If I see a cop car, I will know you told, and then you know the deal: You watch me kill your father, watch me torture and kill your children—*our* children—and then I torture and kill you. Remember, I will go down in a blaze of glory—I PROMISE—don't dare me or think me incapable."

Mom was inside the hospital and figured that if he were going to kill her whether or not she went to Florida, then it wouldn't make a difference if she reported him now. She had just seen the triage nurse when she felt the vibration of her cell phone. She'd been surprised when he gave it back to her, but now she understood; it was so he could text her. There were three consecutive messages that went something like this:

START TEXT
"Do you know where your daughter is? I do."
END TEXT

START TEXT
"You tell, she dies. Daddy's next."
END TEXT

START TEXT
"I will then immediately drive to Connecticut
to kill your son. Do you read me?"
END TEXT

Mom told us that she went into the bathroom at the hospital and was able to move her nose back in place without the doctor's help. She could live—or die—with an ugly nose. What she couldn't live with was the potential sacrifice of Raymond or me. That's what my father counted on, and both of them knew she would do his bidding.

CHAPTER TWELVE

February 18, 2008

*"And he seized the dragon, that ancient serpent,
who is the devil and Satan . . . and threw him into the pit,
and shut it and sealed it over him . . ."*
—BOOK OF REVELATION

Mom woke abruptly the next morning when my father grabbed her ankles and yanked her out of the bed she had slept in down the hall from their bedroom. She frantically tried to kick free of his hold while screaming at him to let her go—but of course he didn't. He grabbed his Glock and dragged her down the stairs. She scrambled to her feet only to find the gun pointed at her.

"You're going to Florida."

Her body still ached from head to toe from all she had endured the day before, but adrenaline had kicked in when he was dragging her down the stairs and she ran to the back door. He twisted the knob, yanked the door open, shoved her outside into the misty, drizzling rain, slammed the door behind her and relocked it. She knew he could just as easily unlock it and kill her right there, so she sought what protection she could from the rain and freezing cold. She hurried beneath the deck and sat on the hose reel. She pulled her cell phone from the bra she wore at night to keep it hidden on her, just as Patrick had instructed. She held on to it like the lifeline it was.

As she huddled there, cold, wet and shivering, she wondered if she could make a run for it and not be gunned down in the process. My father liked his cat and mouse games. Knowing him as she did, she was quite sure he was watching from a vantage point that would enable him to shoot her if she came out from her hiding place. She didn't think it would be an instant kill with a clean shot through the head or the heart. That would be too easy. He would first want to play with her for a while. He would wing her enough to bring her down, quickly and efficiently gag her to silence any screams, then drag her inside to amuse himself until he was tired of the game.

She thought about his kitty kite story and no longer doubted that it was true. Just thinking about his torturing small animals at a time in his life when he was supposed to be innocent freaked her out even more than she already was. She nearly jumped out of her skin when her cell phone rang.

The caller ID let her know it was my father. While she debated about answering, he hung up. He immediately called back. And hung up.

He was toying with her, of course. Ringing and hanging up. Then she thought to silence the ring tone so he wouldn't track her to the deck if he were standing outside. She wanted to call Betsey, her emergency contact, but he had switched from calling to texting. Mom told us they went something like this:

START TEXT
"Where are you?"
END TEXT
START TEXT
"I'm walking the neighborhood." *(She texted back, certain he knew that was a lie.)*
END TEXT
START TEXT
"If you don't go to Florida, I won't let you back in."
END TEXT

Mom had to think about that. Was there a possibility he would find some fun in being magnanimous for a moment, just long enough to let her back in while he went about packing and expected her to do the same? She thought back to the phone calls at work, and how he liked to keep her off balance, but not so much that she got fired. That would ruin one of his favorite mind games.

To make her escape she needed the cash she'd managed to save and hide. She needed her car but it wasn't going anywhere without the key she'd had made and hidden. *Thank you for that, Patrick,* she thought, since my father had confiscated the only ones he thought she had. She also needed a coat and at least one change of clothes to get out of her miserably wet, cold pajamas—not to mention the need for shoes.

Everything she needed was inside the house. So were the tickets to Florida. He really wanted to go and killing her here would potentially mess up those plans, so maybe there was a chance he was counting on her cooperation. She thought that if she played along, maybe that would buy her enough time to get what she needed and she could at least try to escape. There were a lot more maybes than the one certainty she had—the time was now or never. She was cold, she was wet, she was petrified, she was panic-stricken, she was shaking and she had no clue what she was going to do, but Mom texted him back.

```
START TEXT
"Okay, I will go to Florida."
END TEXT
```

He let her back in on his terms and that included her making him coffee before he took a shower. The whole scenario was bizarre, with Mom going through the motions in soaking wet pajamas, bare feet nearly blue from the cold, and hair coated in melting ice crystals. Equally surreal was his cheerfully whistling his way to the shower. She was thankful for the length of time she could count on his spending in the bathroom—at least an hour.

She changed clothes, pulled the secret spare car key from its hiding place, and drove to Betsey's house, which was about six minutes away. She remembered too late that she had forgotten the hidden money.

"He's going to kill me," she said between sobs while Betsey gave her tissues. "I have to go home and get the money before he gets out of the shower." Betsey said later that at this point my mom's whole body was shaking. Mom *knew* that she was going to die.

"Why? You have the car, don't worry about the money. Why don't you just run now?"

"Because he'll find me. I know he will. Remember when I was

here yesterday morning? " Mom had gone to Betsey's house early the previous morning, before my father got up and they left for Connecticut. They were working on a plan of escape when her cell phone rang. It was my father. Betsey pleaded with her not to answer, but instead, she put him on speaker so Betsey could better understand what she was dealing with.

His voice roared through the receiver and a chill filled the air. "If you don't get home right now, I'm going to find Jennifer, take care of her, then track down your baby boy in Connecticut and finally take care of you."

At that moment, something in Betsey's eyes changed. My father's cold, frightening voice caused Betsey to realize what danger Mom was in. But despite her urging her to stay, Mom had gone back home

Now, at this moment, Betsey again, for the second time in two days urged her to stay. But Mom felt that she had to go back for the money and for the safety of Raymond and me, because he knew where we were and how to get to us. Yet her mind kept repeating: *Don't go back! Don't go back!*

Mom's reasoning skills were not operating correctly—terror can do that to a person. Unfortunately, hindsight is always 20/20 and on February 18, 2008, there would be much that she would come to regret—starting with the fact that she never should have gone back to the house.

Betsey Torres, Barbara's friend and co-worker:
I worked with Barbara at IS 364 in Brooklyn, New York. Barbara was the secretary at the school and I was a School Aide. Our desks faced each other and we worked very closely together. As the years went on,

Barbara and I became very close friends and we slowly began to confide in each other.

I met her husband at a school party, but only saw him a few times after that. The night I met him, I thought he was very possessive of Barbara. She didn't leave his side. She didn't socialize at all with me or the other people from the school. She just sat with him and hardly got up from her chair. I felt that he was very odd and I felt bad for Barbara that night.

I saw bruises on Barbara all the time. She would wear scarves on her neck and long sleeves when it was 90 degrees in the school building. I observed bruises on her face, arms, neck, and hands. Once she had a sling on her arm and I can recall at least five times that she came to work with at least one black eye. Another time she had stitches on her face when she came home from a vacation. I also noticed her limping on different occasions. There were several times that she would wear a lot of face makeup and sunglasses.

I tried for a few years to speak with her about what was going on in her life, but she never opened up to me. I let her know that I was her friend, a person she could trust and count on, and I promised to be there for her if she ever needed to talk. She would just say, "Things are hard at home" or "My husband works long hours and sometimes he gets frustrated." After the trip to Jamaica in the summer of 2007, Barbara began to open up to me. I begged her to tell me what was going on and why she was so sad all the time. One day, I believe it was in either August or September of 2007, she just totally fell apart and began to slowly tell me how bad her life was at home. She told me how many years her husband had been abusing her and how bad the abuse was, both physically and emotionally. She told me that she was worn down and burnt out and she was terrified that he was going to kill her one of these days. She told me how she worried about her children. Jennifer had lost a lot of weight and Barbara was sick over this and very concerned for her daughter. I also knew that Raymond was very, very quiet and

Barbara worried about him as well—was he holding shame inside, or was it anger or fear?

Barbara also told me about Ray's sexual perversions. She told me how it disgusted her and how horrible it made her feel. But she was happy with the fact that he didn't "touch" her any longer. She told me they hadn't had sex together in a very long time, so at least she couldn't get sick from his deviant behavior.

I spent several hours a day with Barbara at work and I saw her crying many times. Her husband would call constantly—all day, all the time. He would scream at her through the phone and although I could not hear his exact words, I could hear the tone of his voice through the receiver and the frightened look on Barbara's face while she was on the phone. She would hang up crying, only to have him call back again and again and again. Sometimes she would go to the bathroom to wash her face and compose herself and when she returned I would have to tell her that her husband called three more times while she was away from her desk. It was very hard to see Barbara like this, since she is such a sweet and kindhearted person.

The episodes became more intense between December 2007 and February 2008. It was so bad that Barbara and I worked out a code so that I could be sure she was okay when she was home with him. When I was worried about her I used the code that went like this: I would call her house and ask to borrow $50 until my next pay check. If she answered and things were okay at home she would say, "Sure, I will bring it tomorrow." If she didn't answer, she would always call back within ten minutes since she knew how worried I was and say that she would bring it tomorrow. If she said she couldn't loan it to me, that meant things were bad and I would call several times until I got the okay answer.

I was petrified for her. There are so many stories of men killing their spouses and I was afraid she was going to become a statistic. I knew the hundreds of phone calls he made to the school through the years, and how

209

he would scream through the receiver while Barbara was working. I knew how he continuously called back if Barbara told him she was busy, and how he would stalk her by telling her where her car was parked, that she better watch her back when she left work, that he was leaving the kids home alone when they were younger and going out. All these things frightened me and they were escalating at this point. I couldn't imagine how they frightened Barbara.

There were several episodes that were very bad, such as her return from Jamaica. However, February 17 and 18, 2008, had to be the worst. Barbara was an emotional wreck. She could hardly breathe, she wasn't making much sense and she was totally beside herself with worry. She felt she could not go to Florida alone with her husband—he would constantly tell her stories about cops that got away with murdering their spouses (or whose wives were never to be found) and he swore that would happen to her one day. I was so worried about her in that house and with that man.

The day before the incident, Barbara came over to my house in the morning totally and completely incoherent. She cried and cried and cried, telling me that she was sure he was going to kill her in Florida if she went. She said she couldn't go but she didn't know what she was going to do since he was threatening to harm her children and her family if she didn't go. I tried to convince her to stay with me, but she was so scared of what he would do to her children, her father and herself if she left that she couldn't do it. Again, I explained to her how I felt and that my house had an open door policy for her and her children if she needed me. She thanked me but went back home that day promising to call me later to let me know how things were going. When I heard from Barbara that evening she was in St. John's hospital emergency room. Her husband had punched her in the face and she believed that her nose was broken. She was waiting to be seen by a doctor, but her husband was threatening her and harassing her. I didn't hear from her again until the following day when she came back to my house at approximately 11 a.m., and I have never seen Barbara in the frame of mind she was in at this time. She couldn't talk, she sobbed, she shook, she was an emotional wreck and couldn't even express herself. She was scared, really, really scared—terrified! Then she remembered the money she left behind. The money she had been saving since Patrick told her it was her only way out. "I need to go back, Betsey, and get my money. I need that money to leave, to get away." So Barbara left. I cried when she left and felt in my heart that I would never see her again. At that moment, I was sure he was going to kill her. I waited about an hour and a half and then started my frantic "I need to borrow money" phone calls. I called her house phone twice and I called her cell phone twice. She never called back. It was at this point that panic set in. I picked up the receiver and dialed 911.

"What's your emergency?" "I believe that my friend's husband has killed her." A short while later my sister came flying downstairs to tell me to turn on the TV and look at the news. This is how I found out that she was not dead—that he did not finish off the task that he so freely threatened her with.

When Mom got back to the house from Betsey's, my father was still in the bathroom. Mom estimates that she had been gone for approximately thirty to forty minutes, but can't be sure, since her frame of mind was completely unstable at this point. She needed to pass the bathroom door in order to get to her bedroom and retrieve the money that she kept hidden in her underwear drawer. As she passed the bathroom door, she knocked and told him something about needing to run an errand prior to going to Florida. Her thinking was that if she told him she was leaving the house, he would be less likely to come and try to find Raymond and me immediately. This would allow her the time to get the message to us that she was leaving our father for good.

He opened the bathroom door, grabbed the gun he had placed on the bathroom sink, aimed it at Mom's head and screamed that she was not allowed to go anywhere. He then stared at her with a blank look that literally sent shivers up and down her spine.

Mom was a mental, emotional, and physical mess as she frantically ran to their bedroom to grab the money hidden in her drawer. She attempted to calm down. She had to think. She thought about me—that it was crucial she call me at work and warn me not to come home—that I must immediately seek some protection from my father. She wasn't sure what kind of protection that might be, but she knew that I needed someone or something to stand between him and me if he came to my job or came after me when I arrived home. She thought about my brother. She must call his school—tell him not to come home, not to answer his father's phone calls. Protection was also what my mom needed in order to get out of there. And there it was . . . protection. My father's *little* gun, the .38 that he wore strapped to his ankle, was just laying there.

For more than two decades she had begged him to stop leaving his guns around and now, in her frantic state of mind, it occurred to her that a gun could be her ally. Arming herself seemed to make sense. She couldn't believe that she had not thought of it before.

This time could be, *would be,* different. Her thought was to scare him, and to give her the courage to pass by the bathroom without fearing the gun he would no doubt aim at her—and to once again leave the house; this time with her money.

She lifted the .38 and instantly hated how it felt in her hands. With only the clothes on her back and the wad of cash in her bra, she wouldn't be taking a suitcase anywhere—not to Florida and not to wherever she ended up once she made it past my father. She still had her pink fluffy slippers on—she hadn't even realized that she had worn them to Betsey's house. It was too late to get shoes now. She was walking quietly past the bathroom when the door jerked open.

"Going somewhere?" He aimed the big gun—his precious Glock—at her forehead.

His face was expressionless. His eyes terrified her; they were blank, they showed no emotion—they didn't look human.

Then she remembered the little gun was in her hand. But she couldn't move. Couldn't aim. She started to cry.

"You're. Dead." He took a step closer. It was at that precise moment that she knew my father, her husband of 24 years, was going to kill her. She knew her life was in immediate, imminent danger. She was as good as dead.

A gun went off. It sounded like a sonic boom ricocheting off the tiles. At first Mom saw nothing, felt nothing. Then she saw him. He was sliding down the shower door, a smear of blood behind him.

"Oh my God! Ray! Oh my God!" *God help me, please. Help him.* She dropped the little gun that she must have shot him with and moved toward him.

"Let me help you!"

Then he laughed and tried to get up, lifting himself with the palms of his hands. He looked toward his big gun, the one he had just aimed at her head. It was on the floor. He was getting up, reaching for the gun on the floor as he screeched, "You're going to fucking die! Blaze of Glory, bitch!" He kept repeating, "You are fucking dead! You are fucking dead."

This time his long reach couldn't help him and his screaming threats wouldn't stop. Mom knew he was about to kill her with his big gun. She knew her life was going to end at that moment—but then she beat him to the Glock. She couldn't think past the sound of her own panting, or the threats that my father was spewing at her. She closed her eyes. A shower of shells hit her face. Finally, my father stopped screaming at her. That's when she opened her eyes.

My father wasn't yelling at her. He was no longer trying to get up. He wasn't threatening her any longer. He wasn't moving.

My mom wasn't dead—my father was. In a matter of seconds, three lives were saved and forever changed.

Epilogue

Among those testifying at the trial were my mom's friend, Betsey; my Aunt Robin; Ronald Ferrara, who was in Jamaica with my parents; Jesse; Valerie, the safety officer from the school where Mom worked; Mom's friend, Tania; several expert witnesses; Mom, Raymond and I.

At the end, right before the verdict was read, I couldn't even breathe. Raymond told me that it felt to him like time had stopped. We were both so scared and nervous. Hearing "not guilty" for murder in the 2nd degree and again "not guilty" for the first gun possession charge was the most ecstatic feeling either of us have ever had.

Then the verdict of "guilty" on the possession of a second weapon was read and we were confused. We had been told that if she were found not guilty on the murder charge, she would be found "not guilty" on the weapons charges. I am still confused . . . I don't understand how a self-defense verdict of *not guilty* could be reached, but there could be a *guilty* verdict from using the weapon she used to defend herself.

Mom is at home, awaiting appeal of that charge. She lost her job with the school because at this point she is a convicted felon, and even though this guilty verdict is being appealed, the City of New York let her go. But even with all that has happened, her personality is emerging. She is becoming the person my Aunt Robin and Uncle Michael remember before my father took her dignity and self-respect from her. She used to be jittery and nervous all the time, worrying about setting him off, or having to call him or text him. She seems to feel safe now—she doesn't have to worry about pleasing him all the time. Before it seemed as though she wasn't her own person—that she didn't have her own personality—but now her laughter is beginning to return and she smiles again.

I am married now. It was a long time before I would trust Jesse—or anyone. Jesse is really patient and understands that I have been through a lot. It's difficult to think about having children. I am still having a hard time with all of this. Would I really want to put kids through that?

Jesse Joyce, Jennifer's husband:

I remember Jennifer's father as being quiet and cold. He would often fight with Jennifer and didn't seem to get along with Barbara's family.

The night of Jennifer's 21st birthday party, Barbara was extremely upset. Ray verbally abused her at the end of the party, along with Jennifer, and continued to do so on the way home.

Many times, Jennifer was unhappy when I picked her up for dates or went to her house. She would sometimes call and tell me her parents were fighting and she couldn't go out that night. She would be crying on the phone.

The day Ray died, Jennifer called me and said that something had happened at home and she had to leave work. She was upset and thought that her father had done something to her mother. I told her to be careful and meet up with her friend Christie, who wanted to meet her a few blocks away before going home. I wanted Jennifer to understand what was going on before putting herself into a possibly dangerous situation. It was only after she found out what happened that she believed her mother was safe. There was a sense of relief that Barbara wasn't hurt, although there was a lot of emotion, as well as confusion as to what was happening with Barbara and what the future held.

We spoke numerous times throughout that day.

I'm an oncology nurse in San Diego, California. Although I don't see battered women and children every day, I constantly find myself wondering what the patients are going home to. If I see a bruise or a scratch on a patient, I ask questions to see if there might be more that a patient wants to tell me. Whenever a prisoner comes in for treatment my heart sinks with the thought that perhaps they don't belong in jail, or don't deserve to be treated this way.

Raymond's Memories

I have dreams sometimes that he is still alive, doing what he always did—but waking up is a relief. I've been asked how I can stay in the house where he died. It is no longer a house of tension and fear—it doesn't feel like the same house. I don't dwell on what happened to him there, but I do remember the bad memories I have because of him.

It is hard for me to trust people. I thought Vincent, my dad's brother, and his wife, Linda, were on our side. The last few months of my dad's life, they were the only ones outside our home who knew what was happening to us. We were close to their daughter, Kathleen—especially Jen, as they are close to the same age. She called us daily after the shooting and asked about Mom, and came over to the house. Vincent even cried when we told him that Mom was denied bail. Then, overnight, they turned on us. Strangely enough, my dad hated Vincent. He ranted about how fat he was, and how he hated going to his house.

I imagine the change in them was because we didn't go to the funeral. There was no point in going—there was no reason to mourn. Jen talked me into going to the wake. I felt that a wake was for paying respect to someone who had died, and I had no respect for him at all. Jen wanted to go to make sure he was dead—so she could move on and know that he was gone for the rest of her life.

There were some people there from the security company he worked for, but not one cop from the police department came to the wake or the trial. That told me a lot, especially when there is usually a huge funeral with bagpipes and all when a cop dies—but there was nothing for him. According to a cousin of my dad's, there were very few people there. He asked me why Jen and I weren't at the funeral. It was after this when his family cut off communication with us.

I hate that I have my dad's name. I've thought about changing it, but I can be myself—having his name doesn't mean that I am anything like him. I am not like him and I don't want to be like him. I am now engaged to Shannon. She is very supportive and understands everything that I have been through. She is always there for me. I am looking forward to the day when we have children and I can give them a better life than Jen and I had. I am very excited about that!

I've been asked what advice I would give to kids and women who are in a situation such as ours. I'm afraid that once it gets to a certain point, as it was with my mom, there is not much that can be done except try to stay hopeful—hopeful that he will change; hopeful that he will leave you alone; hopeful that good will prevail.

My advice would be prevention before it gets that bad. Read the signs of abuse. If someone is trying to control you—if they want to know where you are all the time—get out now! This also includes anyone who is in a potential relationship, such as dating. Parents need to teach their children this; teachers need to tell their students this; anyone who can positively affect a child's life should be communicating to them the warning signs of domestic violence.

Because we were afraid to tell anyone (I couldn't even say in the confessional what was happening to us), our strength came from within ourselves through prayer, love, hope and strength—for which I am thankful to my mother, who instilled them in me.

__Christie Gallagher, Jennifer's friend and neighbor from across the street:__
I have been fortunate to know Jennifer since I was about four years old, and as a long-time friend I have seen her unhappy many times. As we were growing up I thought her feelings were typical teenage emotions. However, I occasionally experienced the severity of control that Ray had over everyone in the house. During our adolescent years, I witnessed an example of his harsh physical and verbal discipline when Jen acciden-

tally dropped their puppy. I remember how he yelled at her and commented about her being "stupid." When it happened, I immediately left Jennifer's house and went home with an uneasy feeling. I was astonished that her father had become so distraught with Jen about an incident that seemed so minor to me.

Because I was in Jen's house on a frequent basis, I was under the impression that her father was very strict about how things were, but I was a young child and didn't realize that his demeaning behavior toward Jen was a constant occurrence. Unfortunately, it never occurred to me that someone was affecting her well-being. Although Jen and I always had a very close friendship, I didn't know what she was experiencing every moment that she faced her father. To this day, it is unsettling for me that I didn't realize something was wrong. After becoming aware of the abusive person Ray Sheehan was, I feel sad and angry— but knowing that Jennifer lived each day fearing for her life is most disturbing to me.

The day that Ray Sheehan died will always be a vivid memory. Every detail of that entire day, especially Jen's emotions, will never be forgotten. I was upstairs in my house and as I looked out of the window, I saw Jen's aunt running toward the Sheehan's house. I shouted downstairs to my father and said, "Did something happen by Jen's house?" At that moment, I instinctively knew that something was wrong. I remember thinking that someone may have gotten hurt. I was very unsure about what could have happened, but I just knew that something had gone terribly wrong. I was very frightened, thinking that something may have happened to Jen or Barbara. I was trembling as I ran out of my house.

When I arrived outside Jen's house, I was told that Ray was dead. I was shocked and couldn't even imagine what had happened inside. As the cops closed in on the block, everyone became franticly worried about Barbara. As the commotion continued, I tried to remain focused on finding Jen to make sure that she had support during this terrifying time.

Her family told me that she was working and would be coming home shortly. I was relieved to hear that she was not in the house, but I continued to worry about her. We were all in a state of panic, but I knew that Jennifer had to be informed of what had happened. I was afraid that she would hear about it and would have to travel home in terror of the possibilities.

After receiving permission from her family, I called Jen at her job and asked her to come home. All I could do was put myself in her position. I knew I couldn't tell her that something happened in her house and expect her to remain calm, so I fabricated a story, hoping that she would leave work and come home. When I finally reached Jen at her job, I was so nervous I didn't know what to say. I tried my best to tell her the story I had made up to lessen her stress, but she was uncertain and very concerned about why I was calling her at her job. Although I thought I was calm and composed while speaking to her, my anxiety was apparently obvious and Jen knew that something was wrong. She continuously asked me where her mother was and asked me to go to her house and stay with her mother until she got home. Speaking with her was very difficult, and I remember feeling nauseated. I kept thinking that Barbara was going to be escorted out of her house in handcuffs at any moment and Jen was not yet aware of what was happening.

When Jen got closer to home, I met her taxi a few blocks away from her house. As soon as I saw her she frantically asked, "What's wrong, what's wrong? Where is my Mom? What did he do to her? Please tell me that my mom is okay!" When I saw Jen's face and emotions, I was overwhelmed with feelings of anxiety, fear, and sorrow. I didn't know what to say to her, so I just continued to give the taxi driver directions to Jen's Nanni and Pop's house. As soon as we got out of the taxi, Jen dropped to the ground and began to cry hysterically. I can clearly remember her saying, "Where is my mother? Is my mom hurt? Did he hurt her? Take me to my mother!" Jen insisted on sitting on the ground until I promised her that everything was okay. I was able to assure her that I *knew for certain that Barbara was safe. I wasn't sure what I should tell her about what had happened, so I avoided details. At that point, all I knew was that Barbara was placed in the police car and Ray was dead. Because Jennifer was crying and pleading with me to tell her what had happened, I told her what I knew. Every time I relive that moment, those same feelings of nausea and sadness come over me. Jennifer's fear for her mother's life was heartbreaking.*

By the end of the day, Jen was reunited with her brother and other family members. I will never forget the concern that she and her brother, Raymond, expressed for their mother's life. The most terrifying event of that day was the fact that Barbara, a loving and kind-hearted woman, was arrested.

Fortunately, their lives are being restored and they no longer have to live in fear of what might happen to them.

Contact the authors at:
P.O. Box 140423, Station B
Howard Beach, NY 11414
RJB@inbedwiththebadge.org

APPENDIX A

A Letter to
Our Father's Family

The hurt and pain you have caused in our lives, as well as in the life of our mother, is immense. You have chosen to lie and accuse us of lying without any facts to verify your standpoint. This is a terrible thing you have done to us. We could never imagine treating *anyone* this way, least of all the people we care about.

Vincent, we will never understand what you have done, other than you chose to take the easy way out of this situation. It is easier, after all, to blame someone else than to admit your own brother has horribly abused his family. Unfortunately, we weren't granted an "easy way out" when our father was beating our mother day in and day out while threatening to kill us if we told anyone. And, for the record, he would have killed us.

Your "family pride" is obviously more important to you than the truth. We cannot fathom that just because he was related to you, his horrifying, monstrous and terrifying acts could be ignored. It takes a courageous and genuine person to admit that one of his own has done wrong and to support his victims. It's clear that you do not have these qualities.

We are proud to say that our mother, and both of us have told the truth and nothing but the truth. We knew the facts and we laid them out for the jury to judge. You will never be able to say the same, because your allegations were not facts, but mere guesses and lies.

After our mom told you the horrendous seriousness of the situation and how fearful we all were, you did absolutely nothing. You didn't even do anything to help your own brother, whom you are now so "proud" of, understand how sick he was. We would hope that you have the conscience to feel shame for this—but even if you choose to continue to lie, God knows the truth.

The hardest part for us through all of this is that you have let us down. We trusted you; we believed that you were looking out for our best interests, as was everyone else in our family. We were badly mistaken. We wonder how you might feel if your own daughter or grandchildren were in our situation? Would you sit back and do nothing? Would you champion their abuser? Would you sit and laugh from your side of the courtroom at their expense? We never knew what you were laughing at, but God knows, nothing about this situation is funny.

We will be able to live the rest of our lives knowing that we spoke only what was honest and truthful. You will have to live the rest of your life knowing that you were dishonest, and that you supported someone who abused his wife and young children. We hope that when you go to sleep at night this sits heavily on your mind, because we will never be able to get back the eighteen years of our lives that your "loved one" took from us.

Linda, you stood up at our mother's sentencing and judged her with such conviction, knowing that you weren't speaking the truth. Keep in mind that one day you will be judged in the same manner by God—only He knows all truth.

—Jennifer & Raymond

"I've learned that people will forget what you said, people will forget what you did, but people will never forget how you made them feel."
—Maya Angelou

Why This Case Is Important

Holly Maguigan,
Professor of Clinical Law, New York University
Co-counsel for the Defense in the Barbara Sheehan Case

The common stereotypes, misconceptions and myths surrounding domestic violence and battered women—that they are to be found only in low-income families; or among people of color; or in families where there is job-related stress or any other major stressor; or that abused women are young, timid, or not competent—were all challenged in the Barbara Sheehan case.

One of the reasons there was so much attention from the press over this case is because it did not fit these stereotypes. From outward appearances, this white, middle class family seemed typical of many families. Barbara and Ray both had good jobs. Both of their children had been high achievers—model students, in fact, and were attending college. Barbara had always been involved in her church and in her children's activities. These are all measures of stability. It is amazing that Barbara Sheehan could have endured such harrowing violence over such a long period of time and not only held a job, but was able to function at all. This is definitely inconsistent with the stereotypes. It tells us that domestic abuse can take place anywhere—and it can happen to anyone.

This case was important on another level because Ray Sheehan was a police officer. Although we would like to think that someone who appears to be a successful police officer could not possibly be violent at home, it happens. There is no special immunity for those who have sworn to protect and serve. A man's record as a law officer may be exemplary, but his actions at home tell a different story. Ray Sheehan was one of these men.

Another aspect of law officers as abusers comes when a battered woman, regardless of her husband's work, seeks help and protection from the police. If an officer who is abusing his own wife answers the call, he would certainly not see this woman as the victim. There is distrust of police officers among many women because of the way they are treated—more attention is given to the batterer than to the victim. The women make statements such as, "I didn't like his questions." "I didn't like the way he responded to me." "I didn't trust him."

The Barbara Sheehan case illuminated the importance of an entire defense team. I have worked with Mike Dowd on other cases, and when he called me about this one, I didn't hesitate. I didn't even know what the case was about when I said yes. I admire the way he works. He is remarkable in that he puts together an entire defense team of people who will look at the case with fresh eyes and possibly from a different perspective from his. It is not about making a name for himself; it is about doing the best job possible for his client. He welcomes and values the viewpoint of sharp, young people. For the Sheehan case, he asked me to get my law students involved. He has worked with different groups of my students since 1987. Because of all the delays (not ours), and the length of time it took to get to trial, four different sets of students of varied ages took part in the defense of Barbara Sheehan. It turned out to be a compelling case for all of us. The students paid attention—and they were faced with their own acceptance of stereotypes. They went with Mr. Dowd on his first visit to the Sheehan house and saw where Ray Sheehan died.

Some of the aspects of the case that intrigued the students was that Barbara survived this level of abuse. Another was that Ray could have kept all that ammunition in his home—over 700 rounds—and carried at least two guns on him at all times, even after retirement from the NYPD. They were surprised that the prosecution refused to believe that this was a case of self-defense, which it so clearly was, and their attitude startled them. There is a question that all prosecutors should ask in a case like this— "Is this a viable case of self-defense?" This should be an important part of the prosecution's evaluation.

What the students gained from their participation, among other things, was a greater understanding of domestic violence, and how to translate that understanding of what a woman has experienced for the jury; how to prepare for trial; how to put together a case; and, of course, they did an enormous amount of research.

It is not as easy to present a case like this as one might expect. It is hard for people to understand that a situation can get this bad; that it could get to the point where the only choice a victim has is life or death—her life or his life. Any killing is a tragedy, but we all have the right to defend ourselves. People tend to blame the woman when there is trouble in a family. Their thoughts also run along the lines of, "If it was so bad, why didn't she leave him?" instead of, "Why did he beat her?" There are many reasons why a woman might stay in a situation such as this. Fear can keep a person bound. It is a standard threat that he will kill other family members if she tries to leave—*Leave me and I'll get your family (or the kids, or anyone the woman cares about).* She might not want to put her children through a divorce, thinking that it is best for them if their parents stay together. Love can also cause a woman to stay—always hoping that he will change.

The defense for this case was blocked at every juncture, including the disallowance of expert testimony by Dawn M. Hughes, Ph.D., ABPP. Dr. Hughes is a forensic psychologist who has served as an expert witness in numerous criminal cases involving battered women who have assaulted or killed their abusive partners in self-defense. Her testimony was crucial to this case.

Why this testimony would be denied, or why this family that had already been through such terror would be subjected to the additional agony of a trial are questions that can only be answered by the prosecution and the trial judge.

For women who are now living with someone who is abusive, even if it is only verbal abuse at this point, physical abuse is a definite possibility. Muster any resources available to you to keep yourself and your children safe. This is easier said than done. There are local resources and advocacy organizations, but not nearly enough. Get numbers for local hotlines. Educate yourself. The Internet is an invaluable resource. Have a plan—an escape route. Constantly assess the possibility of getting out. Only you will know whether and when that time is right. If it has already escalated to the point where Barbara Sheehan was and you have been charged with a crime in defending yourself, get a defense *team,* not just one attorney. If you don't know where to turn, the National Clearinghouse for the Defense of Battered Women in Philadelphia is a valuable resource for help. Information can be found on the Internet (www.ncdbw.org) or the phone number is 215-351-0010 or 800-903-0111 x3. Collect calls are accepted from incarcerated battered women. Another excellent resource is STEPS to End Family Violence, an unusual advocacy group that works with battered women who are accused of a crime. The website is www.egscf.org/services/steps/ and the helpline phone number is 877-783-7794 (877-STEPS94). If a lawyer won't work with STEPS, I won't allow that attorney to work with my students.

Perhaps you know of someone whom you suspect as living in an abusive situation—talk to her. The hardest cases involve heterosexual adults. Ask her if there is anything that she would like to talk about. Or, be more confrontational and ask what you can do to help her. Tell her you have seen the bruises, or have seen her wearing sunglasses on a cloudy day. But you will have to take the cue from her. She is the one who knows the violence best and will have the best instinct for her situation.

At the time of this writing, Barbara Sheehan awaits an appeal to a New York State intermediate level appellate court on the guilty verdict of possession of a weapon. We are optimistic that this verdict, inconsistent with the verdict that she was not guilty of any level of homicide, will be overturned; that the court will see her possession of the gun as transitory and not criminal, thereby trusting Barbara's account of what took place—she grabbed the gun to keep him from getting it and killing her.

Domestic Violence, How to Get Help, Cops as Abusers, and Other Statistics

WHEN THE BATTERER IS A COP

- Domestic violence is 2 to 4 times more common in police families than in the general population. In two separate studies, 40% of police officers self-report that they have used violence against their domestic partners within the last year. In the general population, it's estimated that domestic violence occurs in about 10% of families.

- In a nationwide survey of 123 police departments, 45% had no specific policy for dealing with officer-involved domestic violence.

- In that same survey, the most common discipline imposed for a sustained allegation of domestic violence was counseling. Only 19% of departments indicated that officers would be terminated after a second sustained allegation of domestic violence.

- In San Diego, a national model in domestic violence prosecution, the City Attorney typically prosecutes 92% of referred domestic violence cases, but only 42% of cases where the batterer is a cop.

Special Problems for Victims

- Her batterer always has a gun (often many guns and other weapons) and is trained to use it.

- He knows how to inflict pain and leave no marks or bruises.

- He's trained to intimidate by his presence alone, and to use his body as a weapon.

- He lets her know he has the power to harm or kill her and get away with it, or have others do it for him.

- How can she call the police? He is the police!

- He tells her that if she does call police, the officers (his colleagues and friends) will believe him and not her . . . and he's right.

- He often threatens that if she reports to police he'll lose his job, and if that happens, she's dead.

- He has access to surveillance tools like phone taps, police scanners, vehicle tracking devices, and audio and video recording equipment to stalk or monitor the victim's activities.

- The batterer or his fellow officers will often "patrol" the victim's house, work place, children's school or daycare center.

- Friends, family and service providers are afraid of the batterer and thus afraid to get involved.

- Domestic violence advocates may share her information with the police. (Other than Purple Berets and Women's Justice Center, all domestic violence advocates in Sonoma County work for either the police or district attorney's office.)

- He knows the location of battered women's shelters.

- He knows the court system, often testifies in court, and knows district attorneys, judges and bailiffs personally.

- Jurors assume police officers would not lie in court.

If Your Batterer Is a Cop

- Even more than other battered women, when you decide to leave or prosecute you need to move strategically and get good advice from the outset.

- Find an advocate who is independent from police agencies and experienced in working with police officer violence.

- Make a comprehensive safety plan: put money aside he doesn't know about, identify where you can flee with your children, etc. Domestic violence shelters can help you with this anonymously.

- While the tendency is to take "baby steps: so as not to enrage him, once you make your move, the more power you can muster, the more likely you can stand up to the power you'll be up against. Report to police or district attorney, get a restraining order and report to his police agency all at once.

- If police and DAs are unresponsive, go to the press.

- Contact Purple Berets for "Police Domestic Violence: A Handbook for Victims."

This information was gathered from the **National Center for Women and Policing, Life Span, and Abuse of Power**. www.purpleberets.org/violence_police_families.html

The following is another good source for this type of information: www.sfgate.com/cgi-bin/article.cgi?f=/c/a/2012/01/14/MNFQ1MP92G.DTL

THE COLD, HARD FACTS

- One in every four women will experience domestic violence in her lifetime.[1]

- An estimated 1.3 million women are victims of physical assault by an intimate partner each year.[2]

- 85% of domestic violence victims are women.[3]

- Historically, females have been most often victimized by someone they knew.[4]

- Females who are *20-24 years of age* are at the greatest risk of nonfatal intimate partner violence.[5]

- Most cases of domestic violence are never reported to the police.[6]

1. Tjaden, Patricia & Thoennes, Nancy. National Institute of Justice and the Centers of Disease Control and Prevention, "Extent, Nature and Conse-

quences of Intimate Partner Violence: Findings from the National Violence Against Women Survey," (2000).

2. Costs of Intimate Partner Violence Against Women in the United States. 2003. Centers for Disease Control and Prevention, National Centers for Injury Prevention and Control. Atlanta, GA.

3. Bureau of Justice Statistics Crime Data Brief, *Intimate Partner Violence, 1993-2001,* February 2003.

4. U.S. Department of Justice, Bureau of Justice Statistics, "Criminal Victimization, 2005," September 2006.

5. U.S. Department of Justice, Bureau of Justice Statistics, "Intimate Partner Violence in the United States," December 2006.

6. Frieze, I.H., Browne, A. (1989) Violence in Marriage. In L.E. Ohlin & M. H. Tonry (eds.) *Family Violence.* Chicago, IL: University of Chicago Press.

www.ncadv.org/files/DomesticViolenceFactSheet(National).pdf

Signs of Abuse

If you answer yes to any of these questions, you are likely to be in an abusive relationship:

- Do you feel like you are walking on eggshell to keep the peace?

- Do you feel like a prisoner in your own home?

- Does your partner hurt you with bad names and put-downs?

- Does he threaten or harass you?

- Give you "the look"?

- Shove, slap, or hit you?

- Abuse your children?

- Keep you from seeing friends or family?

- Destroy your property"

- Hurt your pets?

- Does your partner follow you, spy on you, or show up at your job, school, or friends' homes?

- Listen to your phone calls or keep you from using the phone?

- Does he force you to have sex when you don't want to?

- Accuse you of having affairs?

- Control all the money and give you little or none?

- Keep you from getting or keeping a job?

Adapted from the National Coalition Against Domestic Violence (www.acadv.org/facts.html)

BATTERED WOMAN SYNDROME

According to a prominent expert on battered women, Dr. Lenore E. Walker, a woman must experience at least two complete battering cycles before she can be labeled a "battered woman."

The cycle has three phases. First the tension-building phase, followed by the explosion or acute battering incident, then the calm, loving respite—often referred to as the honeymoon phase.

The four general characteristics are:

1. The woman believes it's her fault

2. The woman's inability to place the responsibility of the violence elsewhere

3. The woman fears for her life and/or her children's lives.

4. The woman has the belief that the abuser is omnipresent and omniscient.

Women need to know that according to research spousal abuse does not typically stem from a problem with the relationship, but instead begins with the man's emotional insecurities, low self-esteem and abusive behaviors witnessed in his childhood.

Reasons Women Stay

There are many reasons a woman would stay in an abusive relationship. Among them: reinforcement during the honeymoon stage after being beaten, loss of self-esteem, women feel they are the peacekeepers in a relationship, adverse financial consequences, threats from the batterer to kill self or children, learned helplessness.

Many of these women still love the abuser even after they leave, by whatever methods. But they must understand that in order for the battering spouse to change he must go through a two step process to get help for his abusiveness.

First he must suffer negative consequences for the violent behavior and then he must go through specialized spouse abuse counseling. If drugs or alcohol were involved he must also be treated for the addiction.

The batterer must believe and accept these five concepts:

1. Accept responsibility for the abuse

2. Understand the use of abuse to control partner

IN BED WITH THE BADGE

3. Understand the level of emotional dependency on the part of the abuser

4. Gain the ability to recognize low levels of anger and to use anger management techniques

5. Have empathy for the victim

Legalities of BWS

Let's examine the legal implications of BWS. Battered Woman Syndrome was first proposed in the 1970's. According to Joe Wheeler Dixon, PhD, JD BWS appears to be the product of legal advocacy and not science. BWS seems to owe its existence to the needs of legal advocates to support and justify claims by battered women who have killed (their batterers).

The defense revolves around the woman's mental deficiency and helplessness. Learned helplessness can be induced in lab animals, but no sudden rage or aggression.

So, a battered woman kills her abusing husband. She doesn't do it during a beating, thereby being able to claim self defense; she probably can't, he's too strong.

While he is awake and watching her, she suffers from learned helplessness; he has brainwashed her into thinking she is helpless and worthless. She perhaps kills him in his sleep because that's the only time she can overpower him.

This is where the Battered Woman Syndrome came into play. Her defense claims it was a form of self-defense. Where one might agree with that, the fact is she took a life. He received no trial for his crime. Perhaps she did what she felt she needed to do, but she must also take responsibility for her actions.

In court, expert testimonial regarding domestic violence can by used for various purposes: to demonstrate the defendant is a battered woman, to explain an abused woman's state of mind and/or conduct or to support a claim or the validity of a particular defense.

Experts have acknowledged that Battered Woman Syndrome is considered a subcategory of Post Traumatic Stress Disorder, but not a mental disease in the context of insanity.

According to Mary Ann Dutton, Ph.D.'s "Critique of the Battered Woman Syndrome" Expert testimonial concerning battering and its effects cannot adequately rely on a single construct such as Battered Woman Syndrome: the comprehensive body of existing knowledge cannot be so condensed. Instead, focus should be on identifying the specific questions relevant to the issues at hand for which there is a body of knowledge to support a valid conclusion.

Effects on Children

What effect does Battered Woman Syndrome have on children? An authoritative study states that children who witness domestic violence but are not battered themselves show behavioral and emotional problems similar to those experienced by physically abused children and may also suffer from Post Traumatic Stress Syndrome later.

One study states that witnessing violence between parents is more of a predictor of future violence than being of victim of child abuse.

The children see that this behavior is acceptable by their most important role models. Boys learn that battering is a way to influence loved ones, without being exposed to more constructive alternatives. As they grow up, boys tend to identify with their fathers and lose respect for their mother or feel guilty for not being able to protect her.

Domestic violence becomes a factor in custody cases. Psychological studies have demonstrated three reasons why the battered woman is more likely to be a better custodial parent than her abusive spouse:

1. The abuser's violence damages the emotional health of the children

2. Placing the children with the abuser perpetuates the cycle of violence

3. The mother's parenting skills are probably better since she was likely to have been the primary parent.

We've all heard about cases where the battered mother did not protect her children from abuse by the batterer. In one case the expert described Battered Woman Syndrome as "a breaking down of a woman's self confidence and self respect to a point where she no longer knows if she is crazy or not." BWS was used in one case to demonstrate that the mother did not have the ability to protect her child from the father's sexual abuse.

Once outside of the abusive relationship a woman can overcome the feelings of inadequacy and helplessness that were brainwashed into her while being in an abusive relationship. Courts have granted modification of a consent decree to change custody from father to mother when the mother later was able to demonstrate that the consent decree was signed under duress, that the father battered her during the marriage and he used inappropriate discipline with the children.

Even when children are not physically harmed in domestic abuse, the negative effects are complicated and long lasting.

For more information, contact www.selfdefense-4-women.com/battered-woman-syndrome.html

What Are the Treatments for Battered Women?

Treatment for battered women, or as follows:

1. Get out of the home at all costs. Be prepared to live with a peer, or family member. Take what is emotionally meaningful or sentimental. The rest can be replaced. It may take years, but eventually you can replace it. They are ONLY materialistic items.

2. Obtain a restraint order. The responsibility is now yours to implement it. So many times the perpetrator begs, cries, asks for forgiveness, uses the children as a go-between, any ploy they can conjure get you back. DO NOT SUCCUMB! Call the poli   your restraint-order power.

3. Inform your place of employment. These men will usually approach you at work. Make calls at work, and even try to sabotage your employment.

4. Seek out a good therapist. You may have to go through one or two until you find the right one. Please stay in therapy. This is a long process. Remember, you have been abused for a long time; therapy will not just take a few sessions.

5. Take care of your children, see if they need a therapist, and monitor their grades from school. Depending on their age, they will have a hard time asking why they cannot see Daddy.

6. Empowerment. You must slowly get strong, trust your decisions, and realize your talents. You have been emotionally beaten down and possibly physically beaten. You have God-given talents; begin to recognize them and push forward.

7. C. Hurn says, "The past is the past, that is why they call it the past." Yes, one must look at the past and then learn from it, but to ruminate and dwell on it is counterproductive. There is a new path ahead of you that YOU and only YOU created. There will be a time when you can walk it safely and be happy. I promise you.

8. All forms of healing are at your fingertips. It has been shown that putting in place a variety of treatment modalities has the best outcome. Medication is very helpful if not life-saving in the short term; spirituality, therapy, and group work is very powerful—here you are face to face with other women who have been through this hell. YOU ARE NOT ALONE!

9. Chances are, because of the abuse you have lost some of your friends, or have not been in contact with them. Give them a call. You have freedom now, move forward with your independence.

10. Say hello to your parents again. Re-introduce yourself to your parents. They have been outside observers and chances are you have not shared with them the truth. Enjoy your family, they will want to be with you, spend time with you and love you.

For more information, contact www.peaceandhealing.com/psychology/battered-woman-syndrome/

DOMESTIC VIOLENCE STATISTICS

- Every 9 seconds in the U.S. a woman is assaulted or beaten.

- Around the world, at least one in every three women has been beaten, coerced into sex or otherwise abused during her lifetime. Most often, the abuser is a member of her own family.

- Domestic violence is the leading cause of injury to women— more than car accidents, muggings, and rapes combined.

- Studies suggest that up to 10 million children witness some form of domestic violence annually.

- Nearly 1 in 5 teenage girls who have been in a relationship said a boyfriend threatened violence or self-harm if presented with a breakup.

- Everyday in the US, more than three women are murdered by their husbands or boyfriends.

- Ninety-two percent of women surveyed listed reducing domestic violence and sexual assault as their top concern.

- Domestic violence victims lose nearly 8 million days of paid work per year in the US alone—the equivalent of 32,000 full-time jobs.

- Based on reports from 10 countries, between 55 percent and 95 percent of women who had been physically abused by their partners had never contacted non-governmental organizations, shelters, or the police for help.

- The costs of intimate partner violence in the US alone exceed $5.8 billion per year: $4.1 billion are for direct medical and health care services, while productivity losses account for nearly $1.8 billion.

• Men who as children witnessed their parents' domestic violence were twice as likely to abuse their own wives than sons of non-violent parents.

From http://domesticviolencestatistics.org/domestic-violence-statistics/

OTHER WEBSITES OF INTEREST

Olson Center for Women's Health: www.olsoncenter.com/home/index.php?option=com_content&task=view&id=137&Itemid=31

Every 9 Seconds: www.every9seconds.com

STEPS to End Family Violence, an unusual advocacy group that works with battered women who are accused of a crime. The website is www.egscf.org/services/steps/ and the helpline phone number is 877-783-7794 (877-STEPS94).

National Clearinghouse for the Defense of Battered Women in Philadelphia is a valuable resource for help. Information can be found on the Internet (www.ncdbw.org) or the telephone number is 215-351-0010 or 800-903-0111 x3. Collect calls are accepted from incarcerated battered women.

About the Authors

Jennifer Barbara Sheehan was born on April 28, 1986. She attended Our Lady of Grace Elementary School and was very active in softball, basketball, and gymnastics. She went to St. Francis Prep High School from 2000 to 2004, where she participated in gymnastics and cheerleading and was a eucharistic minister.

Jennifer met her current husband, Jesse Joyce, a pilot in the United States Navy, at St. Francis Prep while they were both students there. She attended Molloy College from 2004 to 2008 and graduated with a Bachelors degree in Nursing.

While she was in college, she coached gymnastics at Cherry Lane in New Hyde Park and worked as a nursing assistant at Memorial Sloan Kettering Cancer Center. She passed the N-CLEX in June of 2008 and became an RN. She then worked at Memorial Sloan Kettering Cancer Center in their Urgent Care Center as an RN from 2008 to 2010.

Jennifer and Jesse got married on July 3, 2010. Following the wedding, they moved from New York to Jacksonville, FL, and then to San Diego, CA. They currently live in San Diego, where Jennifer is a registered nurse administering chemotherapy at the University of California San Diego. She also volunteers there with victims of domestic violence, and is pursuing her masters degree in Nursing.

Raymond M. Sheehan is the son of Barbara and Ray Sheehan. Raymond is currently working in the New York Public School System, and is pursuing his master's degree as a physician's assistant. He and his fiancée, Shannon McCoy, plan to be married soon.

Raymond lives in Queens, NY, in the same house he grew up in. He is co-author of the book *In Bed With the Badge*.